THE
CHEATING
WIFE

Roni,
Stand Strong!
Love,
Shelly

by Shelly Snow Pordea
© 2024 LBB Publishing Co.

Cover art by David Hayward

Special thanks to editor and friend, Lindsay J.K. Nichols

Paperback ISBN 978-1-962417-01-3

Ebook ISBN 978-1-962417-02-0

Praise for The Cheating Wife

"A compelling–and educational–masterpiece! Stitched into excellent storytelling is a subtle but devastating narrative that will ultimately open eyes, minds, and hearts. Countless women will identify with Morgan whose plight and determination will continue to inspire long after the last page has been read. *The Cheating Wife* shakes the unethical foundations of systems that need deconstructing and offers inspiration for how we, as a society, can and must do better." – Gerette Buglion author of *Writing to Reckon*

"Too often, those who experience domestic abuse are unseen and unbelieved, abandoned to pick up the pieces of their lives without support, even in the evangelical church. *The Cheating Wife* shines a light on the nuances of these experiences and how they impact individual lives. From the beginning, I was rooting for the protagonist, Morgan, as she reminded me of many women I've known. Morgan and her two children struggle through perhaps the most difficult time in their lives but are ultimately resilient in this story of survival and freedom." –Cait West, author of *Rift: A Memoir of Breaking Away from Christian Patriarchy*

"Shelly skillfully blends the safety of a fiction story with the unfortunate truth and consequences of manipulative, toxic relationships in *The Cheating Wife*. A thought-provoking read, this relevant tale reaches into your heart with empathy and understanding, leaving you better for reading it." – Jen Burns, author of *James and the Big Battle: A Children's Book about Allergies* and *Helping Your Kids Be Creative and Change Their World*

"I was hooked on this story from the first page! The character layers and the way the story builds...I can't put it down. From the complex characters to the fascinating storyline, this is a must-read!" – Breanna Kleeschulte author of *The Business Betty: A Coloring Book for Business Badasses*

"Shelly had me completely immersed in *The Cheating Wife's* world from the start. She paints the external and internal world of Morgan so well, which is essential to understanding the nuance of marital abuse. Stories like Morgan's need to be shared for our culture to better grapple with the aspects of abuse that are not 'extreme' and therefore, not always visible. This story will make many women feel seen, and hopefully, better supported." – Mattie Jo Cowsert, author of God, Sex, and Rich People: A Recovering Evangelical Testimony, Coming Fall 2024.

"*The Cheating Wife* readers are immediately drawn into a web of suspense and pool of secrets from the very first page. As the plot unfolds, the twists and turns keep readers on the edge of their seats, making it impossible to put down. Perfect for a weekend binge-read." – Taylor Thompson, Best-selling Author and Host of the internationally ranked High Performer Podcast

CONTENTS

DEDICATION

To the group of women whose lives inspired the stories sprinkled throughout these pages: your courage, resilience, and strength give me hope.

CONTENT STATEMENT

This book contains scenes that address sensitive and potentially distressing topics, including but not limited to adult themes, emotional trauma, and interpersonal conflicts. If you may be triggered by discussions of sensitive subjects, such as abuse or other challenging situations, please consider your well-being before proceeding with this book. Practice self-care and reach out for support if needed.

In the United States:
National Domestic Violence Hotline Hours: 24/7.
Languages: English, Spanish and 200+ through interpretation service
1-800-799-7233 or SMS: Text START to 88788
Website: https://www.thehotline.org/
For the Suicide and Crisis Lifeline dial 988
Available 24 hours. Languages: English, Spanish.
https://988lifeline.org/

"When a woman starts to disentangle herself from patriarchy, ultimately she is abandoned to her own self."

~ Sue Monk Kidd

Chapter 1
Afterglow

Something about starting a new day gives one hope that life is meaningful, and missing a moment longer than absolutely necessary would be unforgivable. That's how Morgan Connor used to feel about mornings. For years, she made a habit of getting up hours before everyone in the house, sipping her coffee, journaling, and soaking in the quiet, magical moments of the sunrise. But she had been out of her regular rhythm for a while, finding it difficult to rise naturally. That morning, sunlight peeked through small slits of barely-opened blinds and shone onto Morgan's face as she curled her toes, tucking them under the corner of the comforter that had ridden up past her ankles overnight.

"Ugh," she whispered as she tugged. "You blanket hog."

Morgan spoke playfully, but no response came from the other side of the bed, so she assumed Jarvis was downstairs already, making her uneasy about trying to sleep in. Even though she hadn't been well enough to spring out of bed every day, Morgan was still sure to be the first one up, if only a few minutes early. Setting a positive tone for the kids was high on the list of priorities, and that meant getting Jarvis his cup of coffee and playing soft music throughout the house. If he started well, everyone had a better day. Not that he was the volatile type. He wasn't. His rage would come in whispers. In laughs. In snide and cruel comments that would never make one cower in fear of getting hit, but would tear at the very fabric of a soul.

"Jarvis?" she called out sleepily. "I'm getting up now...promise," Morgan said loudly enough for him to hear, but careful to not wake the kids.

Letting teenagers sleep until the very last minute was *always* a good idea.

When no answer came, Morgan rubbed her eyes, stretching her feet and arms out across the bed before that feeling came. The one you have when you can sense something coming, or perhaps is already there, like an intruder who has broken in overnight, but is indisputably uninvited. She tried to shake it off.

"Honey?" she called out, waited for a second, albeit impatiently, but didn't hear the slightest sound in response. Panic began to set in as she rolled over, casting her eyes toward the clock and springing up out of bed.

"8:43? How did I sleep so late?" she consciously said to herself. "Kids? Jarvis!"

Her voice was loud and frenzied as she jolted through the house, room after room, shouting.

Making her way into the kitchen, Morgan looked for a note on the chalkboard where the whole Connor family would scribble messages and doodles for each other, but the board was strangely blank. She thought of checking her phone to see if she had any texts.

All four Connors would plug in their phones, leaving them on the counter overnight once the twins were old enough to get their own, so Morgan rushed to find hers sitting on the charging station. The notification center scrolled on and on. Eighteen calls, twenty-four texts, Instagram DMs, emails, and Facebook messages.

"What in the world? I don't even remember what I posted," she thought.

She tapped on her missed calls, trying to breathe steadily and stave off the rising heat that started in her toes and made its way to her chest before wrapping itself around her entirely.

"Think positively, live positively," Morgan reminded herself audibly. Without taking the time to set her day up for success with a morning routine, she felt the threat of the emotional tornado she usually suppressed attempting to surface.

Six calls were from Tiffany, the best friend a girl could ask for. From the time they were young girls, Morgan and Tiffany shared everything. Clothes, makeup, secrets, occasional crushes (as long as they were celebrities) but never, ever, boyfriends. Tiffany knew everything about her and was the one person in the world Morgan could absolutely trust. She didn't take the time to fully read any of Tiffany's texts, knowing it would take too long, and simply pressed the icon to call her back.

"Tiff?"

"Mo, where are you?"

"What do you mean? I'm home. What is going on?"

"Oh, Morgan..." Tiffany's voice trailed off as she let out a heavy sigh. "Have you been on social media yet?"

"Today? No, I just woke up. I've been so out of it lately. I think Jarvis took the kids to school and let me sleep in..."

Morgan let a pensive moment slip between the words in their conversation, reminding her that thoughtfulness toward her growing fatigue was not in Jarvis' character, but she quickly brushed it aside. "He's never done that before...but he didn't leave a note or anything."

"Oh, sweetie, he left you a note all right."

"What?" Morgan's mind wouldn't let her begin to process Tiffany's vague implication.

"Look, Mo, I need you to make yourself some coffee and stay off your phone. Can you do that for me?"

"I mean, I guess. I have a ton of messages and stuff. Did something happen at the school?"

"Listen, do you trust me?" Tiffany kept her voice low and calm.

"Why would you ask me that? You know I trust you...and now you're just scaring me."

"Okay, that's fair. I *do* know you trust me, but I'm asking you to wait for me to get there. Then I can explain things to you in person. There's a situation, and I think I need to be with you before you learn it somewhere else, do you understand?"

"Why would I understand that? Please, Tiffany, just tell me what's going on right now."

"Look, I'm getting into my car. Can you hear me?"

Morgan heard the phone click to a blank, dead sound before it connected to Bluetooth and Tiffany's voice came through over the car speakers.

"Okay, Mo, you there?"

"Yeah, I'm here. It's going to take you at least ten minutes to get here, Tiff. Why can't you just say it? Tell me what happened. I can't..."

Morgan's breath control wasn't where it needed to be, but it was better than it had been in the past. Even though she was convinced that no therapist would ever be able to help her prevent the panic attacks that had plagued her everyday life for years.

"It's okay, Mo," Tiffany reassured her. "You're going to be okay."

Morgan couldn't respond as she began to struggle for air.

"Mo?"

"Yes," she finally muttered through a gasp.

"You just breathe. Lie down if you need to. I'm on my way, and I promise you, it'll be all right. I'll talk slowly so that maybe if I do have to spell it out over the phone, I can be at your house by the time I'm done, okay?"

"Okay," Morgan mumbled a breathy reply.

"Breathe in. Breathe out." Tiffany took deep breaths for a few moments, repeating herself, inhaling and exhaling to a rhythm that calmed Morgan enough to speak.

"I'm on the floor," she whispered.

The two besties had done this a hundred times or more and easily fell into their natural pattern. Tiffany was forever the caretaker, and Morgan the one who needed a strong and reliable shoulder. And Morgan knew she was lucky enough to have found it.

"I've got my focus point," Morgan assured her.

She had crawled her way to a large floor rug outside the kitchen and into the spacious living area. Lines in the carpet were fresh as Morgan let the fibers tickle the tips of her fingers. A chandelier above had eight bulbs and four lines meeting at a center point where it held the weight of the fixture, securing it to the ceiling.

"I see the round plate on the ceiling light fixture."

"Perfect. What do you hear?"

"Nothing."

"Not yet? It's okay. Take a second and try again. What do you hear?"

"I hear you breathing on the phone."

"Good. Anything else?"

"Um... The air vents just kicked on. I hear that."

"Okay, good. What do you feel?"

Morgan's hands slid slowly along the soft carpet. "The rug. Pajamas on my skin."

"Great. What do you smell?" Tiffany's words were easy and rhythmic.

Morgan breathed in again, closing her eyes.

"Coffee."

"Perfect. You made yourself coffee?"

"No, I didn't have time. I guess Jarvis..."

"It's okay, let's just finish," Tiffany interrupted. "What do you taste?"

"My nasty morning breath." Morgan let out a chuckle.

Tiffany laughed as she continued in her bestie role, "Yeah, well you'd better get off that floor and brush your teeth in the next couple minutes because my ETA is about six, okay?"

"Okay, I guess I'll see you then." Morgan rolled to the side, pushing herself upward into a cross-legged position.

"Don't hang up. Just stay on with me. I'll be there in five."

"Well, I don't think you want me to brush my teeth while you listen."

"I don't mind. You brush, I'll talk. ETA is four."

Morgan laughed under her breath. "You're just making me believe minutes are passing like seconds," she replied, knowing Tiffany was using a countdown method they had both learned in therapy.

"You're too good to me, you know? I don't think anyone deserves such a high-maintenance friend. Especially you."

"Nah, of course, I do. People with a long fuse need a lot to burn, am I right?"

"Oh, please. I've seen you when your fuse isn't so lengthy, that's for sure," Morgan reminded her.

"You're not wrong," Tiffany chuckled. "You're certainly not wrong about that."

Tiffany and Morgan knew each other like no one else knew them, not family, not spouses, not a single soul. The secrets between them were as intertwined as the redwoods. Roots so enmeshed they could look down sometimes and forget where one began and the other ended. Not entirely visible to the casual passerby, this bond, but *they* knew...even though the lives they lived were seemingly opposite.

Anyone would have thought growing up they were two peas in a pod, destined to be carbon copies of each other. Morgan and Tiffany were expected to follow a path they were surely destined for. But, like most expectations, that's not how things turned out.

Tiffany was broad-shouldered, loud, and funny, with stunning tattoos down her right arm that she would cover at work and home, but would proudly display during nights out in the city where few knew her. She wore her hair in a faux-hawk-teased bundle and pierced herself on whims. The little girl who had grooved to the music of dance recitals from the age of seven had abandoned makeup, costumes, and anything too traditional to embrace her fun-loving style. She never married and wished only to be known for her work. Why she had never left the small town of St. Clair was a mystery, but Morgan couldn't help but secretly blame herself.

She was the needy one. The one who kept the prim and proper rules, married a doctor, took her kids to sports events and dance classes, and posed for pictures at every charity event from the suburbs to the city. From the outside, this town would assume Tiffany was the woman likely to fall apart at the seams and Morgan was as steadfast as the sunrise. Though Tiffany could lose her cool about a grave injustice when they were in their twenties, she had learned to regulate her passions and go with the flow. It's likely the reason the community didn't completely force her out. She may not have looked the part of a loving caretaker, but she sure acted it.

They shared another laugh as Morgan walked upstairs to the master bath, let the water run, and grabbed her toothbrush.

"Okay, are you going to just let me brush my friggin' teeth while you listen to me spit, or are you going to start spilling the beans?"

"Hey, I'll be there in three, so it's up to you. I can start now and finish when I get there, or you can tell me about your plans for the day in between brushes."

"Well, that's not practical," Morgan sputtered with a mouth full of toothpaste.

"Fair enough. I'm pulling into your neighborhood now. Seriously three minutes from your driveway."

"Speaking of which..." Morgan peered out the bathroom window as she noticed a car slow down in front of the house. "It's so weird. I've been up here for less than a minute and this is the third car I've seen passing my house come to a stop out front."

Morgan moved toward the window to get a glimpse of why someone would want to see anything in front of her house, but she couldn't get sight of much more than a vehicle peeking through the front hedge.

"It looks like they're taking a picture. Geez. Is that what this is about? The freshman dance was at the high school last night. Do they still toilet paper people's houses after those things? Jarvis probably let me sleep in so the twins could skip a lecture, and I'd be the one to clean up a stupid mess," Morgan rambled after spitting and rinsing.

Tiffany was silent on the line, so Morgan continued brushing, letting herself mentally get worked up about the inconvenient turn she assumed her day was about to take.

"Morgan, you still there?"

"Ah hee," she said, hoping Tiffany would be able to understand her words.

"Okay, pulling in now."

Wiping her mouth after splashing water on her face, Morgan took a fresh towel from the drawer and walked closer to the window as Tiffany pulled her car into one side of the driveway, giving Morgan a clear view of her.

"I see you."

Morgan waved towards Tiffany as she put her phone to her ear, stepping out of the car and onto the concrete, and motioned for her to go to the front door.

"Don't use the garage. Jarvis changed the code again last weekend, and I can't remember the new one. I'd have to check my notes. Just come in the front."

"Is the front code the same?"

"Who knows, Tiff," Morgan said with an exasperated tone, rolling her eyes. "You know Jarvis. I'll come down to open it for you."

Grabbing a robe from the back of the bathroom door, Morgan hung up the phone, slipping it into her pocket, resisting the urge to check her other messages.

If it's more than a stupid toilet paper prank, I'll need support to even look at what all these notifications are about. Good thing Tiffany's here. She's always right, Morgan told herself as she walked down the steps, approaching the front entrance.

She unlocked the door and took another deep breath. "Hey, Tiff."

She couldn't help herself. Tears immediately burst from Morgan's eyes as she fell into Tiffany's arms. "What is wrong with me?" she sobbed.

"Nothing. Absolutely nothing, Mo."

"Oh, please," she laughed through her tears. "You know better than that."

"No, I don't. You've been through a lot. And you handle yourself with grace."

"Ha. In public...erm...mostly." Morgan smirked.

The two friends let silence take over a passing moment, trying not to let the heavy truth of Morgan's statement rise all the way to the surface.

"Tell me what this is about, Tiff," she finally whispered as they ended their embrace, closing the door behind them. "I have a feeling there isn't any toilet paper on my front lawn."

"You didn't look?" Tiffany said with a side grin, half-joking.

"Worse. I did look, didn't see any, and still tried to convince myself that you called me a hundred times to see if I needed help with damage control after a stupid prank."

Morgan dropped herself onto the couch in disgust. "See? I'm aware that I'm delusional. How can I *not* ask the question? *What is wrong with me?*"

"Oh, sweetie. It isn't you, and you know it."

"Do I?"

To Morgan's knowledge, Tiffany was the only person on Earth who knew she and Jarvis had their struggles. She started to confide in her bestie cryptically, years after it began. Since his demanding and belittling comments started on the honeymoon, Morgan didn't have the strength to admit to her very best friend that she had made the most colossal mistake of her life. She was hard at work convincing herself it wasn't so bad, that Jarvis really did love her, and that she couldn't possibly be in an abusive relationship. So there was no chance Morgan could be convinced to be honest with Tiffany while she was still lying to herself. But sixteen years in, she had started to come to terms with opening up about her situation, at least with Tiffany.

"Morgan, I know I use pretty emphatic language when it comes to Jarvis."

That made her chuckle. *"Emphatic* is what you're calling it?"

"Okay, harsh, extreme, heavy... Whatever."

They both smiled, allowing another quiet moment to envelop the room.

"And this is about him? What did he do?" Morgan asked as she felt her chest rapidly rise and fall, tears filling her eyes.

She zoomed through a cerebral ticker tape of racing thoughts that might explain an outburst from her husband, but couldn't think of a thing that would have set him off. The house was immaculate, and every handwritten list Morgan had on her desk from Jarvis had been completed. She had learned long ago how to handle most of his quiet rage and psychologically manipulative games. Performance became her forte. When she wasn't alone, that is. Only solitude provided Morgan with a space to let go and face the truth of what her life had become. Perhaps that's why every time she was alone, inevitably the panic would rise and she would seek safety in the comfort of an overly hectic life.

Tiffany didn't speak right away.

"You know the longer you wait, the more my mind spirals, right?" Morgan broke the silence again, trying to remain unruffled as Tiffany moved to the ottoman, sitting knee to knee with her, taking Morgan's hands into hers.

"I'm trying to find the words. And I want to just pull off the band-aid, you know? But..."

"Just tell me he didn't take my kids." Morgan's sobs returned with force as she let her body slump onto the couch, covering her face with her hands.

"No, Morgan. No, the kids are fine. They're at school. He was there this morning. I saw him in the drop-off line."

"You did?" Morgan choked back the tears, sitting upright and wiping her face. "And that didn't strike you as odd?"

"Um, yeah. Seeing Jarvis Connor at 8 a.m. in the school parking lot? Of course it did. That's when I started calling to check on you."

Tiffany was a nurse who spent a few morning hours at the school each weekday while the administration looked for a full-time nurse for the position. She'd stand at the entrance and happily greet as many kids as she could every morning from 7:45 until after 8 a.m. most days. The students adored her, hoping she'd succumb to the pressures of everyone begging her to take the job, but Tiffany wouldn't do it. She was an ER type of gal. The rush of helping people in crises was her addiction.

"And?" Morgan questioned. The pain of waiting was almost unbearable.

"And when you didn't answer, I assumed maybe he *did* just let you sleep in."

Tiffany was the one taking long and deep breaths between sentences, something Morgan hadn't ever seen her do if she wasn't trying to walk *her* through a panic attack.

"But then I got home. And I checked Instagram. That's where I saw it. Actually, when you finally called me back, I was looking for my power washer. I was going to come over and take care of it myself. I assumed you weren't home."

Tiffany was flustered and speaking faster than Morgan could keep up with, especially since she was referring to "it" as if Morgan knew what she meant.

"I'm sorry. I know this doesn't make sense when I am not spelling it out, Morgan. But...it says *cheating wife*...he's telling everyone you're a cheating wife!"

This time, it was Tiffany who was crying. Not uncontrollable, unsophisticated, ugly-cry sobs like when Morgan let loose, but a soft, steady stream of tears.

"He what?" Morgan couldn't believe what she was hearing. "He posted about me cheating on Instagram?"

"Morgan, he spray-painted it on the driveway."

"What? He used the spray paint?" Morgan shouted, jumping to her feet.

This time the rage was hers. A furious scream she couldn't seem to regulate involuntarily made its way from Morgan's gut to her mouth in full volume. She rushed to the garage, searching for the can of spray paint she and her daughter Sadie had used to refurbish a desk. Morgan could picture the solitary can sitting on the garage shelf for the past couple of years. When the twins turned thirteen, Morgan gave them the option to remodel their rooms to fit whatever teenage aesthetic they chose. Milo didn't change much; he'd been adding to his sports wall for years already. But Sadie went all-out with a wallpapered accent wall, bright furniture, and draping cascades of canopy bedding.

"That glowing blue could be seen for miles," Morgan shouted. "Jarvis said it himself when he was making fun of Sadie's design choices," Morgan said as she flung the door to the garage open.

"He *said* that?" Tiffany asked in disbelief as she followed Morgan's percussive pace around shelves that lined the garage. *"To her face?"*

"Heh, yeah. I'm not the only one he tortures," Morgan spoke before realizing what she had said. "I mean, it's not like that. He's not bad with them, I promise. He can just be...blunt. He loves them." She found herself excusing the man even in her fury.

"Oh, Morgan."

"Ah. Here it is!" Morgan said with a jolt as she grabbed a can with an ultra-blue lid and rushed toward the garage door.

"Push the button!" She shouted. She hadn't remembered to open the garage before moving toward the front.

"Okay, okay." Tiffany ran back to the door that led from the mud room into the garage and put her hand over it without pushing. "Don't you want to just get the power washer?"

"No! One more second with those words in the front of my house is too many seconds, Tiff! People are taking pictures!" Morgan's frenzied condition was no match for anyone, not even her calm, cool, and collected bestie.

She crouched down to step outside the still-rising garage door as the buzz of an automatic motor pulsed like a rushing river in her ears. She moved quickly, then froze, standing in front of her very own home, gazing at the accusatory words:

CHEATING WIFE

Methodically, letter after letter, in short, straight lines, Morgan covered the writing with more of the brilliant blue pigment, leaving nothing but messy cobalt blobs on the concrete.

"How many people do you think saw it, Tiff?"

Tiffany stood shaking her head, unable to answer as she slowly approached Morgan, taking her hand and leading her back inside.

"I don't know. But you're going to be okay. I'm here to make sure of it."

Morgan thought back to the previous year and wasn't so sure.

Chapter 2
Prelude to Disaster

"Hey, Mrs. Connor!"

"How's it going, Vanessa?" Morgan smiled at the office administrator as she walked into the front lobby of her husband's practice on a sunny, Tuesday morning.

"I'm doin' just great!"

Vanessa's piercing voice made her cringe, and Morgan mentally recited a quote from one of the books she had been reading. *I am capable of courage and tenacity.* She was committed to self-growth, believing deep down that she could change herself if she just tried hard enough. No doubt the townsfolk would agree. They'd never admit that their favorite trophy wife could be flawed. Even if they saw the crown slipping. Image was everything around here.

Morgan sucked a short breath in between her teeth and mustered up a smile.

"He's in the back. I'll let him know you're here," Vanessa said cheerfully as she moved past the front counter, gliding toward the long hallway of offices. "You on your way to the gym?"

"Oh, no. I'm helping a friend move today."

Morgan clenched her jaw and refrained from excusing the way she was dressed as if she had to apologize for something. It was a baby step toward proving to herself that she was growing past explaining and apologizing for everything. Her therapist would be proud.

"I see," Vanessa replied with a simper.

Morgan returned the grin, attempting to convince herself that Vanessa's kindness was genuine.

"I'll be right back." Vanessa swiped her finger in the air, indicating that she expected Morgan to stay put.

"Actually, I think I'll just head back there myself. I'm sure he's not with a patient yet," Morgan interrupted.

"Oh, um. Doctor Connor isn't fond of..." Vanessa paused. "Well, you would know what he's fond of," she giggled.

Morgan imagined yanking Vanessa's sleek, flat-ironed ponytail and pulling her to the ground in one fell swoop. But she remained stone-faced. She wasn't the type to fight for her man. She hadn't been raised that way. The man fought for the woman. Not the other way around. If a man was flirtatious and over the line, he was touted as charming. A woman could flirt back, only to an acceptable degree. But the woman who couldn't keep her man's eye from wandering? Well, that was all on the wife. Or so she was told. And it went to her bones, that thinking. What proof did she have to the contrary?

Morgan squared her shoulders, allowing the violent thought to turn into a smirk, keeping a quick pace, and making her way toward the back offices.

"I'll just head back there with you," Vanessa insisted. "I have to get a few things before the OAs start to come in," she said as she caught up with Morgan.

Vanessa wasn't the first pretty young woman Jarvis had hired to run his offices since opening the practice, but she was the first one who made Morgan uncomfortable every time she was there. Most of the doctors and every optometrist assistant, or OA for short, who worked with Jarvis were female, attractive, and at least a few years younger than Morgan. Generally speaking, she didn't have a problem with it. But there was something about this office manager that made her crazy. She caught herself holding her breath as Vanessa scooted in front of her with a fast-paced gait, high heels clapping against the tiles with each step. Morgan let out a long sigh.

"Everything all right?" Vanessa asked, making Morgan realize her anxiety was not as well concealed as she imagined.

"Oh, yes. I'm fine. Just trying to let some things go, I guess. I seem to hold my breath a lot lately."

She wasn't sure why she mentioned it, but that was something else Morgan's therapist told her to work on. Over-sharing little things that people could read into. She never talked about the big stuff. She would just ramble on about superficial aspects of life, or break into long explanations with specific attention to detail as if she was teaching a geometry lesson. Her therapist told her it was probably a tactic to avoid speaking the truth about her plight. At least she was working on it.

"I *always* start my day with morning breath work—it's *so good* for the mind and body," Vanessa replied in her typical, chipper way.

She tapped on the door of Jarvis' office, opening it slightly to let him know his wife was there before Morgan could say a word. It was little things like that. Morgan's skin started to crawl and her paranoia began to skyrocket.

"Mrs. Connor is here," Vanessa announced in a near whisper.

Morgan often wished she could be the type of person to demand things. To storm down a hallway insisting she was the wife of the owner and explode into his office any time she damn well pleased. But there it was again. She wasn't raised that way and certainly didn't want to have to deal with Jarvis after a tantrum. It was easier to comply and step back than it was to confront her own monsters.

"Oh, okay, let her in," she heard a voice say.

Jarvis approached the doorway as Vanessa stepped down the hallway to the left, and Morgan moved quickly, allowing a snippet of her frustration to rise to the surface as she forced the door open completely.

"Hey, Morgan!" A familiar, enthusiastic voice greeted her.

Aimee Scott was exuberantly friendly. She never met a stranger, and everyone in the area talked about her as if they would elect her for president. She might as well have been campaigning. Her face was everywhere, right alongside Morgan's husband as the friendliest eye doctor duo in the Midwest. They had partnered early on in their practice and after only eight years had expanded their enterprise to consist of four brick-and-mortar locations and an online eyewear manufacturing and distribution center, as well as creating a certification program for OAs with the local community college.

Nearly half the town worked for the two of them, and it seemed like the other half worked for a megachurch down the road. They were smack dab in the middle of suburbia, where life was meant to be easy, yet never seemed simple. Morgan longed to move back into the city where living may have been crowded and messy but was somehow more livable.

"Oh, Aimee!" Morgan felt a rush of embarrassment flood her face as she stepped toward her. "I didn't realize you two were in a meeting, I just needed to get something from Jarvis.

We didn't have a chance to chat before I got the kids to school and he left for work."

"No need to explain. You're never an interruption," Aimee assured, as she moved in for a hug. "I'll just be in the lobby when you two are finished." Aimee gave Morgan a wink as she closed the door behind her.

Aimee kept an in-home office as well as one at the warehouse, so she and Jarvis would often share a working space at the original practice's location. Morgan regretted not texting or calling and could sense that Jarvis was more than a little annoyed with her. A few seconds of silence expanded the tension as he waited to be sure no one was within earshot.

"What is this about?" he questioned directly.

"I need money."

"What?" Jarvis scoffed brashly, slightly under his breath.

"I don't have any money in my account and can't use my debit card. I was hoping to get Milo the shoes he wanted today after our group helps Rachel move her stuff. We're going to stop for lunch too. So I don't really need that much." Morgan tried to justify her spending, regardless of whether or not she realized she was doing it.

"What the hell do you spend your allowance on?"

"Jarvis, we talked about this. If you insist on giving me money in an account that's separate from yours, then you can't just keep asking me what I spend it all on. It's not fair."

"Fair? Really? You obviously don't have a clue about managing anything, which is why we're in this situation."

"Situation? What financial situation do you think we're in? One where you control me by making sure I only get what you think I should? Do I have to remind you that I was the one who kept our finances in order ten years ago while you were building this business? And God knows what inflation has done to my *allowance*."

She said it like a curse word because that's how it felt. Allowance – noun: a binding, dirty contract that kept Morgan stuck in this situation for good.

"*You* managed our finances?" Jarvis scoffed. "What finances? We were broke!"

"I never once missed a payment. And we were never in debt when I was keeping the books," Morgan reminded him.

"Yeah, well, our expenses aren't what they used to be, okay?" Jarvis said.

"So what? Math still works the same way with big numbers and small numbers, Jarvis. Don't treat me like I'm an idiot."

"Okay. Sure," Jarvis went to his desk nonchalantly and lowered himself to the seat as he rested his elbows on the desk.

Morgan took a deep breath, trying not to lose her cool entirely. She surprised herself at the strength it took to simply manage his unreasonable expectations.

"Jarvis, please. I cannot do this anymore. I try. I really do, but I have to be able to stand up for myself and believe in myself. And I think I've earned at least a little respect from you."

"Why is everything about you, Morgan?" He leaned back in his chair. His condescension blanketed the room as he stared at her, expressionless.

"Are you joking?" Morgan continued mustering her bravery. "I have poured my heart and soul into you and our family over the past sixteen years. I have *nothing* of my own anymore!"

Hot tears began to trickle down Morgan's face.

Jarvis stood without saying a word, moving in close, putting his lips to her ear, slipping his hands around her waist, and hugging her tightly.

"This is why I have to control things," he whispered. "You have no self-control. Just listen to yourself," he said in disgust.

Releasing his grip, Jarvis walked calmly past Morgan as she tried to remember her breathing. He lowered himself to his chair again, reached into a drawer, and pulled a twenty dollar bill out, extending it towards Morgan.

"You're giving me twenty dollars?" she huffed.

"I'm sure it'll cover your lunch. No one ever goes anywhere but that little café on Main after these types of things, and twenty should do it, shouldn't it?"

"Jarvis..."

"I'll take Milo to get the shoes he wants."

"*You'll* take him?" Morgan asked incredulously.

"I'll make sure he gets what he wants," Jarvis replied firmly.

"Just...not what I want," she nodded in defeat.

Morgan wiped the tears from her face, wishing she could summon the strength it took to be stoic, icy, and calculated like her husband.

"It's called an allowance for a reason, Morgan. There are three days left in the month. Buy yourself what you want, just budget accordingly next time."

She snatched the twenty dollars from his grip and he smirked, leaning back on his chair as if on a perch. His grin was nearly pleasant, but something happened to his eyes when he spoke to Morgan in private. It was as if shadows obscured any light that should reflect in his irises, signaling that she had better watch what she did and said. She was glad he had a tell; she only wished she had recognized it sooner. After putting the twenty in the side pocket of her leggings, Morgan turned toward the office door.

"I renewed your membership at the salon last week," Jarvis snarled. "You're looking a little pale, and we have that gala next Saturday. Get some color on your skin, please."

"Jarvis, I hate those spray tan places. I can just wear a long dress instead of a cocktail-"

"No," he interrupted. "The wives wear cocktail dresses. And I wasn't talking about your knobby legs. Your face is completely pale. Just use the tanning bed; it will give you some much-needed sun after this wicked winter and ridiculously rainy spring we've been having. Some women would kill to be taken care of the way I take care of you."

Jarvis rolled his eyes with a huff.

"Anyway," he continued, "I won't have you showing up in a ballgown to draw any desperate attention you may crave."

"I wasn't thinking of a ballgown," Morgan replied weakly, visibly cracking from their exchange and fighting the urge to give way to the rising panic that was coiling around her chest.

"Well, it doesn't sound like you were thinking at all. Especially if you don't have a dress already. You know they have to make alterations when you try to buy off the rack."

"They're fast with them; I have time. Besides, what do you expect me to go shopping with, Jarvis? I'm not able to buy a six-hundred-dollar dress with an eight-dollar balance in my account."

"I'll call the store and book an appointment. You can go tomorrow," he paused as Morgan headed toward the door, hoping to slink her way out.

The only thing she wanted at that exact moment was to be far away from him.

"And get yourself to that tanning bed, seriously." Without rising from his chair, Jarvis raised his voice loud enough for her to hear as Morgan let the door swing shut behind her. "You look ill. It will do you some good."

A group of people at the church who signed up to help Rachel Southers move from her home to an apartment near the town's university were all meeting in a small room of the youth building on the massive church campus. Morgan had made reservations for the group to meet there a week before. She had begun volunteering for the administrative office once the kids started going to middle school. Her volunteer time was the one thing that gave her a sense of ownership. She was good at managing details of events and spent far more hours there than she originally signed up for.

Morgan had put herself in charge of bringing the beverages for the day, and the youth minister, Johnny, met her at the car with a smile.

"Hey, Morgan! Perfect timing. Let me grab those for you." He took the pack of bottled water from the trunk and began walking to the building before Morgan could say a word.

"Well, thanks!" She smiled as she closed the trunk, rushing to keep up with him.

"Oh, of course, my pleasure," he said with a grin. Johnny had a kindness about him that made people of all ages gravitate toward him. The twins had more interest in church after he came along than they ever had before—even as small children when they were excited to attend simply for the candy and snacks.

The two approached the building when Morgan realized she didn't have a key fob to unlock the doors.

"You want me to grab that from you?" she said, offering to take the heavy bottles from Johnny's arms.

"No, no, I have a fob clipped to my belt loop on this side."

Putting himself near the key sensor, he shook his hip to show her, and Morgan let out a little laugh.

"It's right here and extends. It's long enough. Just grab it and wave it by the box. It'll open, I promise." He let out a little chuckle too, as Morgan pulled the fob attached to a retractable cord until it got close enough to see the tiny light flash green.

"Hey, see? It worked. I would've propped the door open between my trips out to the car, but I got *in trouble* last week for it." He rolled his eyes.

"In trouble?" Morgan asked as they walked into the large, open space.

"Yeah, this place is monitored at every minute, it appears."

"What?" Morgan replied. "I know there are security cameras, so... I don't know why I am acting surprised. But how did that get you in trouble?"

Johnny looked at Morgan as if he wanted to say more but wasn't sure if he should.

"Oh, it's okay, you don't have to say anything more if you don't want to," she said uneasily.

"No, it's not that. But a word to the wise. Permission is way easier than forgiveness around here. I know you don't technically work here, but you're around enough that you have to have noticed some things, right?"

"Sure. But I can't imagine that the guy who runs the entire youth ministry would need permission to prop a door open in the buildings he oversees."

"You'd be surprised," he shrugged. And as if he couldn't help himself, continued.

"Apparently, there was an unknown person who came in while we were unloading and I had the back entrance propped open for over an hour. I mean, it was for the spring break carnival that we had to move inside at the last minute because of the crazy weather. I couldn't have the door opening and closing the whole time. We had about twenty-five volunteers or so. Some guy walked in without a lanyard, and the security cameras showed that I was the one who propped it open. Of course, they had footage of me doing that and of this rando entering a while later. My mistake, for sure."

Morgan's eyes widened as he told the story. She had to admit, as a mom, she wouldn't want a stranger just coming into the building for no reason.

"I had a parent freak out when their kid was talking about an older dude she met at the volunteer day. I didn't even notice, so I get it. On me, you know? But there were ten other adults around too. Regardless, there's now a policy about employees leaving doors open. Because that, of course, fixes things."

His tone became more sarcastic and frustrated as he spoke.

"Well, speaking of which, I need to grab my lanyard," Morgan said nervously.

"Ugh, I'm the worst. See? I didn't even notice. But at least today all the volunteers will be over eighteen."

As she turned to go back outside, Morgan glanced at her watch. "I reserved the room from 9:30 and it's 9:15 now. Do they unlock the doors fifteen minutes before or is it ten? I'd rather not stand outside the door waiting to get back in."

"It's fifteen; you should be good now. But don't let in any strangers," Johnny chuckled.

"Got it," Morgan laughed.

She ran to her car to grab the approved volunteer lanyard from the pocket of her driver's side door. She was grateful that the church took such care with volunteers, even though she knew there were always ways for ill-intended people to get around safeguards. Like someone leaving doors open and no one noticing that a person with no business being there had walked right into the bustling space.

When Morgan signed on to help with the church, she underwent a background check, took CPR classes, and attended a sexual abuse seminar. Every volunteer who would be working with children under the age of eighteen had to do the same.

They had a permanent lanyard for all volunteer activities, but on Sundays, when there were thousands of people on campus, every helper checked in at a desk that would print a different colored sticker, changed at random each week.

The sticker included the volunteer's name and picture along with the date—an added security measure she was grateful for. She could admit that she felt safe, both for herself and her children. When the twins started middle school, the security wasn't as high, but there was no reason Morgan ever thought to be concerned for them while they were at church. It was the one place she felt safer than anywhere else in her life.

"Hey, Morgan!" she heard a familiar voice.

"Tiff! I'm so glad you could make it today!"

"Me too! I mean, normally I'd use this time to sleep off a double shift, but I couldn't resist."

"What? Did you sleep at all?" Morgan exclaimed.

"Oh, well, yeah, I totally slept. I got five hours. It wasn't a full double shift, technically. You know how I exaggerate." Tiffany giggled an infectious laugh.

"They made me go home around 3 a.m. We had some trauma victims around eleven last night, so I stayed until everything was stable."

"You're amazing," Morgan said sincerely.

"Ha, I just do my job." Tiffany smiled flippantly and hugged Morgan's arm as they walked into the building together.

Tiffany was a highly respected nurse practitioner. She had won awards for saving the lives of multiple people. She'd been on the news more than once. Between Tiffany and Jarvis, Morgan sometimes felt like she couldn't go anywhere without being with someone whom everyone knew. She was guaranteed to be the sidekick everywhere she went. But, she pretty much preferred it that way. She certainly didn't want to be the recognizable one.

"So, how are you?"

"I'm fine."

"Mo," Tiffany insisted.

She always had a way of getting the truth out of Morgan, knowing when something wasn't quite right. But after having to deal with Jarvis earlier in the day, Morgan was not in the mood to elaborate.

"Really. I mean, even if there *was* something wrong."

"Ha! I knew it," Tiffany interrupted.

"Well, even if there was," Morgan repeated. "I don't think this would be the time or place..."

"In church? Certainly not," Tiffany mocked. "No one's allowed to bring their troubles here," she said as they both walked into the small classroom, laughing. "It's why you don't find me here often anymore," she whispered, tugging at Morgan's arm.

Tiffany had always been the rebellious one of the duo. Not to say that Morgan didn't have her share of sneaking around and breaking the rules when they were teenagers. But even Tiffany would admit to being the instigator. She was the skeptic and Morgan was the one always afraid of getting in trouble. But it was a yin and yang thing. Opposites and balance.

As people began to trickle in, Morgan and Tiffany helped set the refreshments along a countertop at the back of the room, and the coffee Johnny was brewing finished its last bit of gurgling in the percolator.

"Thanks for coming today, everyone," Johnny began. "Feel free to grab some snacks, take a seat, and socialize for a few minutes. We plan to head out in the minibus at 10 a.m., so please make your way to the back entrance on time. There should only be ten or twelve of us today, depending on who is still able to make it. We all know that Rachel is going through a rough patch and we want her and her kids to be loved on. We're family here."

Johnny continued talking as Tiffany leaned in to whisper in Morgan's ear.

"He's cute. How long has he been here?"

"Shush, you," Morgan replied, trying not to draw attention.

"What? You don't think so?"

Morgan gave her a look that Tiffany knew all too well.

"Ha, I thought so. I mean, we're human. We don't have to pretend otherwise just because we're on *holy ground,*" she snickered.

Morgan's eyes widened.

"Sheesh. Don't look at me that way. I didn't say I wanted to jump him."

"Geez, Tiff. Shhhh," Morgan scolded.

But she gave Tiffany a little side eye and they both shared a grin, trying not to break out into obvious laughter.

After their little moment, the women settled into their good behavior, listening to the rest of the instructions before moving across the room to find a seat.

"Morgan, can I ask you to do me a favor when we get back?" Johnny asked as he moved toward the rows of seats.

She nodded. "Sure."

"There are a couple of high school girls coming in this afternoon who wanted to set up for a group activity and I'll need a woman in the building. If you're available, can you stick around until four o'clock?"

"Absolutely," she replied without hesitation.

"Great."

"Mmmhmm, her pleasure." Tiffany quipped.

Morgan was almost sorry she asked Tiffany to come.

***

"Where were you?"

"Oh, Jarvis, I didn't expect you to be in. Sorry. I... I'm a little later than normal," she stammered. "I didn't expect you to be home yet," Morgan automatically apologized, startled at Jarvis' presence.

She had entered the kitchen from the side door, carrying a couple of bags from the day's activity.

"That doesn't answer my question," he insisted.

"I was at the church."

"Until five o'clock? I thought the van was supposed to bring you back to the church at 3:30."

"Yeah, it was. We left a little late, and then Johnny asked me to help out with some of the high school girls setting up for an activity tonight."

"Johnny? Who's that?"

"The kids' youth pastor," she replied with an insulting tone, implying that he should have known exactly who it was.

Regret immediately overcame her. "You know, he's the guy from the East Coast with the dark hair and beard," she said, trying to sound light and cheery to cover up her previous inflection.

"Johnny, huh?" Jarvis asked, raising an eyebrow.

"Yes, I'm sure you remember him," Morgan moved past Jarvis with a bag of leftover snacks, trying to pretend like she didn't know what he was insinuating.

"I do. I remember now. He's a handsome guy, don't you think?"

Morgan's heart flip-flopped from her throat to her chest, and it took all her willpower to keep from shortening her breaths. Questions that Jarvis posed were never innocent, and other than the interaction over the twenty dollars and her allowance that morning, it had turned out to be a pretty good day. She had no desire to ruin it.

Morgan didn't dare let silence slip between them. "I guess," she replied quickly.

She didn't want to say that she found an obviously good-looking man unattractive. She'd learned from experience that such a remark would bring on a bout of Jarvis' reticent fury, so she went with an aloof truth, shrugging her shoulders as she set the treats on the countertop.

"The kids get in at 5:45 tonight," she quickly moved on. "They both have band and swim practice, so dinner will be at 6:15." Morgan could only hope that Jarvis would let it be.

"Okay."

Jarvis moved from one side of the kitchen island to where Morgan was standing at the counter, methodically arranging the snacks into small baskets she had pulled out of the cabinets.

"Maybe we can have Johnny and his family over one night. You know, we can get to know each other," he chuckled, slapping Morgan's butt as he passed her.

Morgan held her breath until he exited the kitchen and closed the door of the bathroom down the hall.

It hadn't always been this way.

CHAPTER 3
PERFECT COUPLE

"M OM, I'M GETTING MARRIED next month."

Morgan lifted her left hand to her chin, resting her elbow gently on the table, as the unobtrusive solitaire diamond caught a trace of light, reflecting the tiniest sparkle.

The shock on Jane Radcliffe's face was replaced with a smile in a millisecond. She had many years of practice hiding her true feelings. Most missed the glimpses of sincerity on her face, giving away feelings that could betray her. You had to be quick enough to catch them. Morgan had learned from the best.

"Oh, baby girl. Look at you, you're beaming." Morgan's mother grabbed her close, pulling her in for a long, tight squeeze. "Congratulations."

"Mom, you can say what you're thinking you know."

"I know, baby. But in a moment of happiness, I'd rather just share your joy. You *are* happy, aren't you?"

"I am, Mom. Really happy."

"Then I'm happy for you," she said, drawing Morgan in for another embrace.

Mrs. Radcliffe had a strange relationship with her daughter. She was fairly easygoing with most people but raised Morgan in a rigid environment with high expectations. Morgan's dad, Charles, passed away when she was thirteen and her mother never remarried. Mrs. Radcliffe wasn't in the habit of allowing even the most devastating event to faze her much.

Financially, Morgan's dad had made sure that she and her mom weren't going to struggle if anything happened to him. Not that anyone can expect a man in his early forties to suddenly die of a heart attack, but he had been judicious in nearly every way. Morgan always saw them as a good match, even if she wouldn't have labeled them as *loving*. One thing she did know was that her dad adored her.

He had good life insurance and set up a college fund the moment Morgan made it into the advanced school program at the age of eight. He was there for each of Morgan's performances and recitals, recording every show and acting as the documentarian for the other kids' parents. He'd share hours of unedited video upon request and made sure that each year, without fail, all parents had a copy of the highlight video he would create for the music and theater programs. In the eighth grade, when her dad died, Morgan had given up the hobbies she loved and plunged head-first into her academic studies.

It was no wonder she got hefty grants and scholarships to attend the honors program of a world-renowned university. With the addition of her college fund, it was like Morgan was getting paid to attend her classes.

By the time she sat across from her mother to tell her she was engaged, Morgan had fewer than two semesters to complete before graduating with a bachelor's degree in chemical engineering. If it had crossed Mrs. Radcliffe's mind that getting married may put a wrench in Morgan's plans to finish school—or pursue her doctorate as she had planned—her mother never voiced an opinion on the matter.

Perhaps it was because Morgan was an only child, or because Mrs. Radcliffe thought Morgan had seen too much trauma in her young life, but it seemed her mother withheld any critique from Morgan if it could be upsetting. Even if her mother's opinion would have been constructive, Mrs. Radcliffe rarely said a word when Morgan would mess up or fall short. She'd simply repeat what the expectations *had been*, and reiterate that those markers were still what Morgan should strive for.

It drove Morgan crazy most days. Her deepest wish was to know what her mother truly thought of her. To understand the person behind the performance. Morgan's rule-keeping—and breaking. Had it ever affected her mom? But Mrs. Radcliffe was an enigma to her own daughter. Morgan considered her to be almost robotic.

She was likely not alone in her desire to see her mother's passion, her anger, and anything that would indicate strong feelings. But after observing other parents in action, Morgan consoled herself with the fact that her mother may not be relatable, but at least she was never volatile.

"Jarvis is a good man, Mom. He's finishing up grad school. He'll probably be done within a year and we'll be able to have a family."

"He does seem like the perfect guy, Gigi."

Mr. and Mrs Radcliffe, a formidable couple in their own right, struggled to have children when they were first married. They had called Morgan *Gigi* since she was a toddler and it remained her favorite nickname. Though she spoke proficiently by the age of two, Morgan showed her age with her glaring mispronunciations, unable to say her full name, Morgan Grace, for years.

She called herself *Go-gace* through preschool and into kindergarten. Her parents spent countless hours trying to teach her to say "just Morgan." Morgan's tiny mouth somehow translated to Gigi.

Mr. and Mrs. Radcliffe found it entirely endearing and began using it as her pet name, reminding her that she could always tell kids her name was Gigi if she wanted to. But Morgan was protective of the name even then and tried her best to say everything correctly, landing on *Oh-gan* until she mastered the full sound of her first initial by the time she made it halfway through kindergarten.

"He *is* perfect, Mom. It feels like he's too good to be true. I don't deserve him, but he'll have me." Morgan leaned her head on her mother's shoulder, desperately wishing she could divulge her secret.

But theirs wasn't that kind of relationship. Mrs. Radcliffe probably thought Morgan would never do anything catastrophic anyway. Morgan imagined that maintaining a pristine image was her stoic mother's main concern and this secret... Well, it might possibly destroy her.

No, the imposing Mrs. Radcliffe didn't need to know. Besides, Jarvis knew. He was there to rescue Morgan from any ridicule or shame she'd confront.

He was nothing less than the absolute best. She was certain of it.

"Morgan, are you sure?" Tiffany leaned forward, taking Morgan's hand in hers and looking closely at the small diamond solitaire on her left hand.

"I mean, you guys are so young. Don't you want to just think about it? Maybe finish school? Move in together for a minute?"

"I knew you'd be the one to push back like no one else." Morgan grinned at Tiffany.

"Because everyone else in this town is crazy, Mo. You know that." Tiffany leaned back on her seat, putting her left elbow on the side of the chair and stretching her right arm to her knee. The sleeve of her shirt moved upward, showing a bit of ink on her wrist.

Morgan grabbed Tiffany's hand and pulled the sleeve up even more.

"Girl! When were you going to tell me you got another tattoo? And how in the world are you going to hide this one?" she laughed.

"Mo, I'm *way* past caring about what my parents are going to say about my tattoos. I stay in this town because of the amazing nursing program, not because these people here deserve me," she chuckled. "And when were *you* going to tell me that you were dating this guy, much less getting *married?*"

"Well... Today?" Morgan shrugged.

"C'mon, Morgan. What's going on? You come home for the weekend, we make last-minute plans, and then you tell me you're getting married? I feel like you don't, I don't know... Trust me? Something's not right here, Mo. And I know it."

Tiffany wasn't wrong, no matter how sorely Morgan wished to object. But she couldn't tell her. Not there. She couldn't risk having a breakdown in the middle of the café.

The three thousand residents of St. Clair City could have been three hundred the way news traveled. They were only forty-five minutes from the city of Minneapolis, Minnesota, where the more widely-known universities were, but it seemed like a whole different world sometimes. Staying in the dorms in downtown Minneapolis had given Morgan a new sense of what life could be.

Once she and Tiffany started college, Morgan tried to convince her to make the move to Minneapolis and commute to the more affordable nursing school in St. Clair, but Tiffany didn't have the college fund Morgan did and wouldn't hear of letting her be the only one to cover expenses. It would have been inconvenient for Tiffany to travel back and forth for work and school anyway, and her life-long bestie knew it.

Morgan wished more than anything that they could have stuck together. She probably wouldn't have been in the same situation had she been able to keep Tiffany by her side, but there they were. Experiencing a form of drifting apart because of the distance...even though Morgan tended to internalize the failing to be her own.

"Yeah, I mean...so much has happened, but...maybe we can go back to your place and talk?" Morgan suggested.

"Nah, my mom's home. I have a feeling you're about to tell me something you won't want the church ladies knowing about by the end of the afternoon," she chuckled.

Morgan picked up the cups and plates as she began stacking everything for the cleanup bin in the small cafe.

"Hey! Don't throw that away." Tiffany protested. "I know you can get your fancy croissants now, you city slicker, but this is the best we've got," she said as she snatched the leftover pastry from the plate and shoved the whole thing into her mouth playfully.

Morgan was always guaranteed a good belly laugh when she was with her bestie.

"Let's just walk to the park," Morgan suggested.

"I'd love that," Tiffany said, moving toward the door and taking Morgan's arm into hers as if they were still two young girls, connected at the hip.

The eccentric little café the two young women had frequented since the time they had pocket change and convinced their parents to let them go unsupervised was right across the street from the civic square and park at its heart. Even though it was technically named Centre Park, locals referred to it as "Central," and the whole town would attend festivals, carnivals, art shows, and an array of other events all year round.

"I'm sure we can find a private spot somewhere. There's not much going on today," Tiffany said, crossing the street, arms linked, walking in step, their familiar childhood cadence

Despite Tiffany's assertion, Central was always bustling. On any given day, hundreds of people would gather in town for a good jog, a leisurely walk, or a gathering with friends. The community wasn't without its charms, but Morgan had become more and more disillusioned with its appeal. What used to feel like home now felt...well, claustrophobic.

"So...?" Tiffany allowed only a few seconds of silence to slip between them before she could help herself. "You know I'm not the most patient person, right? Spill the beans already."

Morgan smiled, trying to find the right words, as she stared pensively at her friend.

"Oh my God. You're pregnant," she blurted out, more loudly than anyone in the county was likely comfortable with.

"Shhh, Tiff, please."

"Oh, Morgan. You do *not* have to marry this guy just because he knocked you up. You know you have options, right?"

"Tiffany, no. It's not like that. Not exactly, and you know I want a family. I didn't plan it this way, of course, but..." Morgan let her words drift into the air, wishing she could control their meaning and, more so, where they'd eventually land. But the truth had been stated, exposed in the light of day.

As the two women stood motionless in the middle of a pathway, a jogger approached, making Morgan feel as if someone had indeed already heard their conversation. Tiffany began searching for a nearby bench.

"There. Let's sit there," she pointed to a bench near the treeline that separated a bike trail from the running trail. The jogger breezily passed by, not indicating the slightest bit of interest in their conversation.

Morgan sighed. "Can I tell you the whole story?"

"I wish you would. You know I will be here for you no matter what, Mo."

"I know. It's just..." Her voice fell silent as they moved to sit next to each other.

"I may not think it's the best idea," Tiffany said, trying to sound encouraging. "Marriage is no solution if you ask me, but if it's truly what you want...I'm here, okay?"

She let Morgan continue in silence, working up the nerve to say the words aloud. They sat on the bench, sharing a glance, wiping tears away, hoping the fresh, fall breeze would kick up.

"Thanks." Morgan sniffled. "I know I can always count on you. I've not made the smartest choices since moving to school. This year has been a little rough."

"Okay," Tiffany responded in a tone that wasn't expectant, just supportive. She waited for Morgan to elaborate.

"Look, you know me. I'm not the partier. But... I don't know, it's senior year, and I wanted to have more of a college experience, you know? There's a whole group of grad students. They're really great. And they throw some pretty elaborate parties."

She let stillness infiltrate the conversation before continuing, hoping that Tiffany would have some sort of reaction, allowing her to confirm or deny her assumptions. But it was clear she was going to give Morgan the time she needed to talk without interruption.

"I had a bit too much to drink." A steady flow of tears began to trickle down Morgan's face. "I didn't know what was happening," she continued through soft sobs. "I don't remember everything."

"Oh, Morgan. Did he rape you?" Tiffany finally asked.

"Jarvis? No. It wasn't him."

"But you *were* raped?"

"I mean, not really. I don't think so. I was drunk. We all were, and we were flirting and kissing. Like, multiple people. But I never wanted it to go that far. I was a virgin, Tiff."

By then, Morgan's quiet, tearful recollection became a full-blown reliving of the trauma that had upended her life, and her shoulders began to shake as she tried to catch her breath.

"Oh, Morgan. Who did this to you?"

"I don't want to say any names. Honestly, I don't know. It could have been any of the two or three different guys there that night."

"Fraternity guys." Tiffany expressed her disdain without reservation. "Were they all there when it happened?"

"I don't remember. It's all so blurry. They were there and then they weren't. We were all drinking, flirting, dancing..."

"Okay, you keep saying that, but it's not your fault. Do you know who you ended up spending the night with?"

"The night? Ha," Morgan scoffed. "It was more like a few hours. There was no one with me when I woke up. I was on the floor in a house I didn't even recognize at 3 a.m. I grabbed my purse. Luckily, it was only a few feet away from me. And I just ran out. My phone was still there. I called a cab once I got down the street, and when I got home I didn't even have underwear on. I was bleeding, Tiff."

Morgan spoke through sobs, trying to say it softly enough not to draw attention.

"Did you do a rape kit?"

"God, no. I was still trying to convince myself that nothing happened. I just showered and got into bed. But the next day... The more sober I got, the more I remembered about the night. Just someone on top of me. Laughing and cajoling. You know, somebody saying, 'You want this, sweetheart, right? You're such a good kisser.'"

Morgan spoke in barely a whisper, unable to continue, hunching herself over her lap on the bench. She buried her head into her knees, placing her hands over the top of her head, hoping beyond hope that no one would pass by.

Tiffany placed her hand on Morgan's back, gently stroking. "It's okay, Mo. We can handle this however you want. I've got you."

As Morgan's breath started to regulate, Tiffany began to speak softly.

"Are you good with me listing out a few options? Do you want me to speak right now, sit in silence, or just drop it for now and move on? I want you to tell me what you think you can handle. I don't want to assume."

Finally lifting herself from the folded position she had locked herself into, Morgan wiped her face and sat up to look Tiffany in the eyes. "They're training you well at that school, huh?" She smiled.

"Yeah, they're known for some good stuff," Tiffany winked.

"Just talk to me. Tell me what you're thinking," Morgan said.

"Well, for starters, we began this conversation with you telling me you are engaged. And that you're pregnant. So, can we start there?"

Tiffany was trying to keep her anger at bay, squelching the desire to rush downtown in a high-speed panic and start demanding to speak with law enforcement.

"Sure," Morgan agreed.

"I think that before you make any life-altering decisions, you should consider therapy. I know a great counselor. She's helped me a lot. Not that you should share a therapist with your bestie. Perhaps that's not the greatest idea, but she'll know where to send you if nothing else."

"I think I'd like that, Tiff. But I'm not going to change my mind. Jarvis knows. He knows the baby isn't his. He was at that party and believed me when I told him everything. In fact, the only reason we're together is because he checked up on me the following week."

"What?" Tiffany looked at Morgan intensely. "What do you mean? He was *there?*"

"Yeah, he said that he saw me and a couple of the other girls leave with three guys we'd been around for part of the evening. He could tell I was pretty drunk and just wanted to be sure I made it home okay."

"And that wasn't odd to you? I mean, if he thought something was off, wouldn't he have tried to step in? Get you away from the people he clearly thought were dubious?"

"I mean, I guess. But he was drinking too. I can't say I didn't flirt and dance with him that night too. I did. It all just got confusing and I must have left. I don't remember anything after the first part of the party and then waking up in the middle of the night in some strange frat house."

"Wait. So, it was a frat house?"

"Yeah. I mean, I think so. That's what it seemed like after the fact. I've never been in a sorority house, but the girls who invited me were in sororities and they live on the street where I was picked up. I assume it's all Greek life over there. I don't pay much attention. I've never been in that crowd, you know?"

"Oh, Morgan. Do you want to go to the police? They could investigate. This is some serious shit."

"No, I don't. Not even a little bit. What I do want to do is put it all behind me. I can't live with this over my head. I have a chance at a good life now, regardless. Jarvis is finishing up grad school, then he has a practicum, and after that, he plans on opening his practice. He's happy to stay in the city or move back to Georgia where he's from. Anything we want-"

"But with a wife and kid in tow?" Tiffany cut Morgan off.

"Yeah. We've gotten so close after this. It's like he's my knight in shining armor, you know? If I'm married, I won't have to go through God-knows-what, and we can just get an early start on something we've both always wanted."

"Morgan, it's the twenty-first century. No one, especially in the city, is going to care whether you're a single mom, or if you give your baby up for adoption, or choose to terminate the pregnancy. You were raped. You have a right to choose what happens to *your* life."

"But my mom. This place," Morgan muttered. "I can't do that. I think we'll make the perfect couple, Tiff. Truly, I do. He's incredible. You're going to love him."

"To the bride and groom," Tiffany chimed as she lifted a glass of champagne, standing in her floor-length gown—something in which Morgan never thought she'd see her best friend.

Tiffany's large, floral shoulder tattoo was on full display, attracting disapproving stares from a much older generation. Her hair was swept up in a half-braid that was gathered to the side and cascaded down the opposite shoulder. Tiffany was elegantly stunning. Morgan relished the fact that she had honest, authentic people in her life who knew the real her, through and through, and still chose to love her.

The three and a half weeks that had passed from the time Jarvis asked Morgan to marry him and their last-minute ceremony, thrown together over semester break, had shown her how a true friend can come through in times of struggle. Mrs. Radcliffe's backyard had never looked lovelier, and the thin white tents cradled a warm glow from the twinkling lights Tiffany and Morgan had hung only hours before. A former colleague of Tiffany's mom had left teaching to become a florist and had called in every favor imaginable.

Nothing was missing, and they were enjoying the intimate backyard wedding of Morgan's dreams. She only wished that Jarvis' mom would have made more of an effort to be there. But she understood. Three weeks isn't a lot of time to change plans and make it to your son's wedding.

As the small crowd of thirty-eight lifted their glasses, Tiffany bent down to hug Morgan's neck as she stood to meet her embrace.

"I love you, Mo," she said with a solitary tear falling down her left cheek.

"Don't you dare cry, Tiff. You know I can't handle it," Morgan replied, falling onto Tiffany's broad shoulder, savoring a brief moment of knowing, standing together in front of their closest friends and family. They were in this for life, and the two of them didn't have to share a single vow to know it.

Perhaps that's the best kind of relationship. One in which there's an obvious lifelong connection. No legally binding act is needed.

As Morgan began to take her seat, Jarvis elbowed his brother, the best man, to take a turn with the toast. Morgan shifted her body, tugging at her gown, hoping to disguise her protruding belly. She suspected it was obvious but prayed most people weren't noticing. The dress she chose was somewhat forgiving, but it seemed like she had a daily reminder that she had not been blessed with a body type that concealed pregnancy. She was only seven weeks pregnant but already felt like she was carrying the weight of a lifetime.

"I hate it when she calls you that," Jarvis whispered into Morgan's ear as his brother poked fun at him from the first sentence of his handwritten speech.

"What?"

"Why does Tiffany call you 'Mo,' anyway? It takes away from the beauty of your name. I love your name. It's distinguished. Dignified."

Morgan smiled nonchalantly, nudging his arm as if to tell him to pay attention to his brother's kind words.

"It's just our thing," she replied. "I like that she's the only one on Earth who calls me 'Mo.'"

Morgan brought Jarvis' hand up to her lips and kissed him softly, then turned her gaze to his brother.

Jeffrey had just begun telling a story about Jarvis using his charm to manipulate neighborhood children into gathering fruit from the trees that lined Apple Blossom Lane, the street where they grew up. Jarvis was nine years old when he bought the fruit for ten cents a piece from neighborhood children, most older than him, and hauled it down to Main Street in his red wagon to sell for twenty-five cents each.

Jarvis set up shop on the corner for a few weekends before someone told his mom, a member of the Board of Education, that her son was selling on the street without a permit. What they thought would result in punishment, or at least a correction of behavior, backfired completely. Emily Connor was nothing if not encouraging of an entrepreneurial spirit. She soon started a petition to allow children between the ages of ten and fourteen to sell their own wares for up to eight hours on weekends without permits. She then helped craft legislation based on the petition. The bill passed before the year ended, just as Jarvis' tenth birthday rolled around. No one ever challenged the law, and to this day you can see everything from lemonade stands to arts and crafts kiosks run by children on the corners of their small, Georgia town on any given weekend.

Everyone clapped and laughed as Jeffrey finished his story about his role as his older brother's grunt laborer and tipped his glass with a wink.

"To my brother, the hardest working guy I know. And the one guy you can never say no to."

The wedding guests smiled and laughed, clinking their glasses together and proclaiming their good wishes for the most popular guy around.

Chapter 4
Seeking Sanctuary

The nature of abuse is secrecy. We depend on it. Not just abusers, but society as a whole. We all want it to stay hidden, behind closed doors, shuffling through dark corridors and into the abysmal recesses of our least-desired thoughts.

Except perhaps for the psychopathic among us, we take no delight in stripping back the curtain to reveal a harmful nature that plagues the human race. Some people will stop at nothing to propagate the idea that there are good people, bad people, and no one in between. We hope to hide the truth of the matter. That it takes all kinds of people to allow abuse to flourish. Enablers. Deniers. Gossipers. The power hungry. The greedy. The fact that somewhere, deep inside, given the right circumstance, these traits could emerge from any one of us haunted Morgan's thoughts. A rage bubbled inside her like nothing she had ever felt.

As she exited the church office, her vision blurred, making the dark halls of the long corridor seem like a fun house rather than a hallway.

"Hey, Morgan. What's going on? Can I help you?"

Morgan heard a compassionate voice from behind as she steadied herself against the wall.

"I...um, thanks. I think I'll be okay, Judy," she replied, turning to see the face of one of her favorite church colleagues offering her consolation.

Judy came closer, extending a hand to Morgan, who looked a little wobbly.

Judy whispered as she put her arm around Morgan, "I didn't think any of it was true. I told Pastor he was wrong. It's not right what they're doing."

"What? You mean..." Morgan could barely breathe, much less find the right words. "He talked to *you* about this? Without calling me?"

"Well, you haven't really been around, Morgan."

"Oh, okay cool. That makes it all right. So much for common decency in the church. No expectation to refrain from 'false witness' and all." Morgan shot up air quotes as her neck tingled with heat.

"Well, Jarvis has been here. I know he's met with the counselors a couple of times. I just thought-"

Morgan cut her off abruptly.

"Really? Judy, do you hear what you're saying? I came here today to ask for help. Thinking that maybe, just maybe, the people I spent time with on a daily basis, for years, would have my back. Protect me from a man who has treated me poorly for years."

The sounds came out faster and louder the more she spoke, like an approaching locomotive. She couldn't permit herself to utter the word "abuse," though. Not there, feeling desperately exposed between the walls she had always thought of as sanctuary.

"That guy on stage, playing those stupid drums almost every Sunday? My husband? He's the one I need protection from, Judy." Morgan shook her head from left to right, waving her hands slightly.

"No, you're right. Of course he didn't stop coming to church after publicly humiliating me. He couldn't risk losing any of his precious and adoring fans."

"Morgan..." Judy looked at her hesitantly, as if she couldn't reconcile the thought of the man she knew with the person Morgan was trying to describe.

"I get it, I do. But think about it. What kind of guy spray paints *'cheating wife'* on his own driveway and then posts it on social media? A guy embarrassed about his wife's infidelity, or a revengeful jerk who is probably trying to divert attention from his abusive ways?"

There. She said it. Jarvis was the abuser. The cheater. The villain. Perhaps she was ready to face it, but it seemed too little and far too late.

Judy's gaze turned from Morgan to the floor and back again as if she was processing data she couldn't comprehend.

"I don't think you're lying, Morgan, but Johnny basically admitted that something was going on between the two of you. And, well..."

"He *said* that?" Morgan interrupted in barely a whisper.

"He didn't say it to me directly," Judy sighed, "but from what Pastor said..." She let her voice trail off, obviously wrestling with what she thought to be true and the story she had heard from those in charge.

"I know it isn't true. Not the whole thing. I mean, not all they're saying. But maybe I can help you, Morgan. With whatever is happening?"

Judy spoke as if she was asking a question rather than making an offer. She wasn't the type to get involved in drama. She'd worked in the church office as the director of administration for nearly twenty years. She had seen people come and go. She'd witnessed minor scandals and major world changes. Her faith and trust in the process, the hierarchy, and the way things were always done was strong. That was true most days, anyway. But this scandal wasn't like the others. This tested her perception of what she *felt* was right and what she was being *told* was right, unlike ever before.

When Morgan first started volunteering, she and Judy worked closely together. After much debate, the Church Board finally approved updating all computer systems within the organization. Soon all two hundred thirteen employees would need to transition their software.

Judy was asked to oversee the project and manage the volunteers recruited to help. At first, Morgan and a few people from the youth group were brought on to help transfer the information. It required hours and hours of data input. Everything had to be read, updated, and properly transferred to new computers. Judy was in charge, but Morgan soon took over organizing the project, never giving Judy cause to give it a second thought. When the project was finished, Morgan didn't stop coming in, even after the last bit of information was entered.

She returned for duty the morning after the office staff threw a thank you party in the lobby for the three volunteers who had holed up in a corner room for two and a half weeks doing nothing but checking and rechecking data. When Morgan continued showing up for work, Judy simply gave her more errands that would eventually turn into essential daily tasks. She began helping out so much that people on the inside and out often assumed Morgan was a full-time employee.

Perhaps that's why she presumed she'd be able to ask for help. Knowing the people within those buildings had spent between thirty and forty hours a week with her for three and a half years was enough to assume people could know the truth about a person, wasn't it?

"Well, Johnny knows exactly what happened, Judy. And whether or not we are friends has no bearing whatsoever on the fact that I never cheated on my husband. With Johnny or anyone else," Morgan insisted.

"I didn't say you did, Morgan. Honestly, I think you're telling the truth. But maybe if you'd have been more open while you were here, we could have helped. And then you just disappeared. I mean..."

Morgan didn't have the stomach to let Judy continue. Judy was acting as if she cared, but Morgan's emotions were too raw to consider that she likely *did* care. By the same token, Judy certainly didn't have the awareness of Morgan's fraught relationship with Jarvis to understand how empty her explanations felt.

And that was intolerable. Morgan was not about to accept the fact that the requirement for helping someone—for showing up for them in their time of need—seemed to be the responsibility of the victim. It just shouldn't matter that she hadn't been around in a while.

"Yeah, you're probably right about that. I don't mean to bite off your head, Judy, but where *the hell* were you a few weeks ago when a scarlet letter in the form of bright blue graffiti turned up on my driveway?"

Judy's eyes widened as they began to well with tears. It didn't stop Morgan from speaking.

"How many phone calls have I gotten from anyone in our so-called community? Do you think it's normal for people to ignore me yet talk to my husband *about* me? Who thought to ask me what might be going on to evoke this much change in my life? Not to mention my children. Has anyone thought of reaching out to them?"

"I'm so sorry you're upset, Morgan," Judy replied through a sniffle.

"Stop. I can't. Keep your apology for my *upset,* Judy. I promise this isn't personal. But maybe it's time you took a long, hard look at how people are treated when they're doing something you judge as wrong. You know, I came here to ask to be paid for my job, something I'm really good at. And what's more, I know you *need* me to keep doing it. How many tasks are undone because I haven't been around in over a month?"

Judy began to open her mouth to respond but let out a pensive sigh instead.

Morgan continued without a beat. "I can't get by without a paid job at this point, Judy. But that doesn't seem to matter, right? If I choose to divorce him, I don't deserve the help. Is it *by the book* for you to treat me like I'm an adulterous woman? Based on what?"

While Judy stood there, receiving the barrage of questions that did not require answers, Morgan paused to get sufficient air into her lungs, then immediately continued.

"And so what if it actually *is* true? What's the worst that could have happened? That I slept with Johnny? Fine. Does that mean it's totally okay for people who say they love and care for one another to do nothing but act like God is judging the wicked now? Take a good, long look. It's not God raining down punishment and wrath on me, it's *people.* And what's worse is that it's the people who say they are called to do *His* work! So, in the name of God, please spare me."

Morgan could barely catch her breath as her body started heaving uncontrollably. She had finally stood up for herself, and regret immediately flooded her heart. Emotions spilling over into a rush of tears, she quickly ran from the hallway to her car, leaving Judy standing in the hallway of a church she'd sunk her life into, stunned and alone.

As Morgan reached her vehicle, she began fumbling for her keys, trying to keep herself from sobbing. But it wasn't grief and sadness that sent her chest into convulsions. It was invigorating relief after expelling all the pent-up words she had finally been able to speak. Not that she was happy she said those things to Judy. But at least her agony now existed outside of her body. That vast expanse could surely contain what had been bottled up for so long.

What Morgan wanted to do was speed away from the church parking lot. Squeal her tires as loudly as possible so someone would know she was making a protesting exit. But instead, she leaned herself against the driver's side door as the gentle mist of an early summer rain began to caress her cheeks.

"Tiff, I need to talk." Morgan couldn't resist dialing when she found her phone instead of her keys. She needed her friend more than anything. "Can you meet me somewhere?"

Tiffany was pretty swift to pick up her phone when she wasn't on duty and would always reject calls when she was, so Morgan was relieved to hear the sound of her voice.

"Yeah, of course, what's going on?"

"I just, I don't know what to do," Morgan said before sliding her body down the side of the car and finally letting out a heavy cry.

She still hadn't found her keys.

"Where are you?"

"Church," Morgan replied, weeping.

"What? Why? Did you go back to work?" Tiffany didn't press but allowed seconds to pass as Morgan's cries became whimpers and her ability to talk regulated.

"Just meet me at Ms. Dinah's, can you?"

"Yeah, I can be there in fifteen," Tiffany assured.

"Awesome. Me too. As soon as I've found my stupid keys," Morgan found the strength to chuckle.

"Oh geez, Mo. I do love you. But you've got to get your shit together."

"Yeah, for real."

Morgan's natural wavy hair bounced and stuck to her face as she walked into the diner.

"Hey," she greeted Tiffany with a solemn sigh.

"Oh my gosh. What happened, did you walk here? You're soaked to the skin."

Tiffany stood from her seat in the corner booth. The one they'd been meeting at since they could ride their bikes and use their allowance money to buy greasy food and milkshakes together. She took her cardigan and put it over Morgan's shoulders.

"No, not the whole way. I never found my keys so I started walking. The Andersons eventually drove by and offered me a ride."

"Well, that was nice. But this AC is gonna make you freeze if you don't dry out a little."

"Good thing you always travel with a parka," Morgan joked.

"Ha, ha. Funny. Make fun of the Florida girl. I'm still not sure why you northerners insist on making it colder inside than it is outside, especially considering the last season we just slogged through. It's crazy."

"You think you'd have outgrown your sensitivity to the Midwest and its way of life by now," Morgan teased as she pulled the cardigan close to her chest and took a seat.

Though the two had been inseparable for what seemed like forever, Tiffany had spent most of her childhood in a suburb outside of Miami. When her parents moved her to the Midwest at the age of eleven, she experienced more than culture shock. The weather was just one of many harsh adjustments she had to endure.

"Well, I haven't outgrown it, and I plan to retire like a normal person and fly south again where I belong," Tiffany smiled.

"Who'd have thought life would keep you here after all these years, huh?" Morgan reminisced as she softened her face into a smile, resting herself against the high back of the booth.

"For real. But we didn't come here to talk about my past. Or my future. Did we?" Tiffany probed.

Morgan shook her head as she leaned against the cushion, slouching to cradle her neck against the back of the seat.

"What happened, Mo?"

"I went to the church..." Morgan let her voice trail off, hoping to find a good way to explain her reasoning to the one woman in her life she knew would *not* understand her constant need to do the right thing in the eyes of the people around town.

"I understand."

"What?" Morgan eyed Tiffany doubtfully.

Tiffany reached her hands across the table to take Morgan's into hers.

"I get it, Mo. I do. I'm not surprised you went. But I'm also not surprised it didn't go well."

"Yeah, I just thought..." Morgan's tears returned in soft whimpers as she tried to wipe them away before the waiter came to offer fresh coffee and take their order.

Tiffany took the lead and ordered a couple of their favorites as Morgan sat silently until the two were alone again.

"I think Johnny told them we are having an affair," Morgan whispered as soon as she was sure no one was within earshot.

"What? Why would he *do* that?"

Morgan looked at Tiffany with a sigh, knowing she couldn't exactly hide the details, regardless of what kind of show she put on for others.

"Oh, Mo," Tiffany paused, leaning back in the booth. "Well, you could have picked an uglier one," she smirked. "I knew you thought he was hot."

Morgan grinned at her bestie's response. The one thing that kept the two of them together like glue was that there was never any judgment. Not even for a situation that society typically judges harshly. Morgan and Tiffany held each other accountable, sure, but it didn't come with condemnation and scolding. It was simply steadfast, loving, and full of understanding. With no false belief that one or the other wouldn't or *shouldn't* fail.

"It's not like that, Tiff. Honest."

"Okay, tell me whatever details you want, but let me remind you of something. It doesn't matter what you've done. There's never an excuse to kick someone while they're down, to bury someone in their mistakes. No matter how much fault they have in it. And sadly, that means Jarvis too. That bastard."

They shared a chuckle and a couple of seconds of reminiscent silence.

"I'm not completely innocent if having feelings for Johnny is a crime. But I promise, I never slept with him." Morgan began wringing her hands while she spoke, resting her elbows on the table, pausing between sentences to sigh. "Jarvis started the rumor, I think. I mean, after his public accusation, he had to have a story, right?"

"Well, sure. But didn't you talk to him after everything?" Tiffany asked.

"No. Don't you think I'd have called you the second we finished a conversation?"

"Good point. So, you really haven't talked at all? For weeks? Is he still in the house?"

"Yeah, Tiff. He even yelled at me for moving all my stuff into the guest bedroom."

"So you're saying you have spoken to each other, just never had a normal conversation. Got it." Tiffany rolled her eyes.

"Yeah, he only speaks if he's scolding me. I'm the crazy one, I guess. He talks in a cool monotone and I've yelled, begged, and thrown things, pleading with him to get counseling with me. But his only response is, 'Why am I going to let the woman who's moved out of my bedroom but not my life demand anything of me?'"

"Wait. He's still in your bed, acting like *you're* the one who's wrong for leaving it? You're joking. And he hasn't told you to move out?"

"Absolutely not," Morgan huffed. "I think this whole stunt was to make me so uncomfortable that I would just leave, you know? Like, he wasn't going to ask me for a divorce, but if he made a public spectacle, it would force me to file. But honestly, I don't want to lose everything. I don't know where to go. What to do. I truly do want to work on our marriage."

"I understand that." For one of the rare times in their relationship, Tiffany felt completely uncertain about what to say. After years of undying support, she wanted nothing more than to tell her dearest friend to cut and run without looking back. But that wasn't Tiffany's style. She believed to the core of her being that people deserved to forge their own paths. As long as her friend told her she didn't want to leave, Tiffany would choose to support her.

"What do you want to do?" she asked.

Morgan shrugged her shoulders.

"I don't know. I mean, with the accusation of an affair... I just don't know. I'm sure Jarvis didn't believe me when I told him I didn't sleep with Johnny. It's not like Jarvis didn't joke about the way I acted around Johnny sometimes. He constantly made little comments about my relationship with the kid's youth pastor. And the truth is, I couldn't argue. I found a lot of comfort in getting close to him. Other than you, Johnny was the one person who let me talk about myself or the kids without any judgment or holier-than-thou advice. He just listened," Morgan admitted.

"I know."

The waiter returned and placed a towering stack of steaming pancakes between them, accompanied by a fluffy omelet, a side of bacon and sausage, and a plate with one large buttermilk biscuit smothered in gravy.

"Oh, geez. I didn't even notice how much you ordered," Morgan laughed.

"Carbs to the rescue, right?" Tiffany winked.

Morgan surprised herself, immediately hungry instead of nauseated at the sight of food, something she struggled with lately. The two friends continued chatting, drowning their woes in syrupy calories, feeling zero regret with their choices. Morgan did most of the talking as Tiffany listened to the details.

Tiffany leaned forward with half a mouthful, practically spitting her food out in protest.

"I'm sorry, you're telling me that you've been asked not to work at the church now? Oh wait, I mean *volunteer* at the church, lest we conveniently forget that you haven't been paid in anything but random gift cards and thank you notes. And Johnny is somehow not affected at all?"

"I guess. I mean, I haven't heard anything, but I haven't been to church in weeks. The kids haven't mentioned it. But I don't know what they're saying now."

"And you've never done anything physical with Johnny?"

"No, not at all."

Morgan lowered her head shamefully. "We probably did cross a line, Tiff. He told me about some struggles he was having. How he was having trouble with his daughter and not getting along with his wife. Then he told me he would date someone like me if we were both single. I'm not saying it was right. But, Tiffany. We knew it wasn't and after that conversation, we apologized to each other and never mentioned anything like it again. We could feel ourselves getting close and just didn't let it happen."

"You mean, it didn't happen during the few weeks between that conversation and when your life conveniently blew up at the hands of a man who likes to pretend you're the villain in this story?"

Tiffany couldn't help but point out Morgan's restraint, knowing her best friend well enough to see that her interaction with Johnny was simply a response to an honest outpouring of attention that she desperately craved and wasn't getting from her partner.

Not that Tiffany thought Johnny was faultless, but she wasn't there to judge him either. If there was one thing

Tiffany had learned in a community centered around the idea that propriety mattered above all else, it was that people do good things and bad things, and it isn't exclusive to one type of person. Human beings are fallible. She was one of the rare ones who didn't act as if it could or should be otherwise.

"Hey, Mom." Sadie poked her head through Morgan's bedroom door. "Can I turn the light on?"

"Oh, yeah, baby. Sorry. I must have fallen asleep."

Morgan had fallen asleep at random nearly every day since *the incident.* She started labeling the vandalism of their front driveway in that manner because articulating any other description felt too agonizing. By the following Monday, Jarvis had paid a guy to power wash the area, but there were still specks of blue that dotted the concrete in places. Tiny speckled reminders of betrayal, and Morgan drove over the surface each morning.

After taking the kids to school, she'd pull into the garage, quietly enter the house, go into the guest room, and pull the down comforter over her head, trying to convince herself that she was only going to take a quick nap.

She rubbed her eyes at the light in the doorway and motioned for Sadie to sit with her on the bed.

"I need you to sign this." Sadie handed her a permission slip for a choir competition the following week.

"Oh, man. I think I signed up to be a chaperone for this," Morgan said hesitantly. "Do you want me to back out of it?"

"Mom, it's been weeks. You have to show your face again sometime." Sadie leaned her head against her mom's shoulder. "We all know this isn't about you," she whispered.

Morgan grinned, pulling her daughter near. "And you wouldn't be mortified to be seen with me?"

"Well, that has nothing to do with gossiping trolls," Sadie quipped.

"Ooh burn," Morgan laughed as she drew Sadie closer, tickling her ribs.

Sadie was a discreetly irreverent type, but not with Morgan. She was more open and honest with her, but sometimes she held her cards close, even with her mom. Sadie was artistic and expressive, but very much guarded with her work. She had written a two-hundred-page novel in the sixth grade, printed it in a six by nine format, cut the pages to size, and watched YouTube videos to learn how to string bind it together by hand. Yet she never once let someone else read it. She told anyone who asked that her novel was "in the editing phase."

It took Sadie a while to warm up to people, but no one would describe her as unfriendly. Surprisingly, she was an absolute natural on stage. When Sadie told her parents she wanted to try out for the middle school musical, they weren't shocked that she was talented or musically inclined. She'd been taking piano lessons since she was five. But to think that she'd be willing to perform in front of an audience was the least believable part. To everyone's astonishment, she belted out the lead role so confidently that she received a standing ovation after her very first number.

Following the show, when crowds were forming in the lobby and admirers were anxiously waiting to offer their congratulations and floral bouquets to the performers, Sadie couldn't be found. She had slipped through the backstage exit and was in the locker room taking off her makeup until someone told her to come join the fun. When she did emerge, she wasn't embarrassed or awkward. She just wasn't expecting gushing compliments to be part of the ritual and shrugged her faux pas off with ease. She was acutely aware of her need for calm, peace, and justice. Sadie was fully unencumbered by the weighty expectations others seemed to find hard to bear.

As Sadie wriggled her way out of her mother's playful embrace and off the bed, she snatched the wrinkled permission slip from the corner and kissed Morgan's cheek.

"Thanks, Mom. Do you want to order dinner tonight?"

Morgan sighed. "Oh, no. I'm getting up now. I'll have something on the table by 5:30."

"Like clockwork," Sadie said, rolling her eyes. "Wouldn't want to piss anyone off."

"Hey-" Morgan was about to admonish her daughter when Sadie continued.

"Just sayin'. We can order out if you want."

"No, it's fine. Really."

"Okay. Oh, and I'll need my birth certificate for our New York trip. There's a meeting next Tuesday and I need two forms of identification. Since I'm fifteen, Mom, I also need to get a passport."

Sadie's tone implied that getting her passport and traveling outside the country was something Morgan had delayed far too long.

Morgan grinned, standing to tidy the bed. She walked towards the bedroom door to join her daughter.

"You don't need a passport to travel to New York," she rebutted.

"You do if you don't have a driver's license. What's a girl gotta do to turn sixteen already?"

Sliding her hand around Sadie's waist, Morgan pulled her in close.

"Oh, sweetie. Please don't be in too much of a hurry to grow up."

CHAPTER 5
HARD FACTS

SADIE USUALLY ENJOYED THE thrill of a virtual reality mystery where she solved a crime or caught a thief red-handed. She loved the rush of exhilaration from the tension of suspense. Not now. Every sensation she was currently experiencing was too real, too tangible. As she closed the door to the credenza, her ears began to ring and all four walls around her began to pulse in an unnerving rhythm. She momentarily lost perception of the exit to her father's office and stumbled to the ground in a daze. Shaking her head and rubbing her sweaty palms methodically on her jeans, she tried to reassure herself that she was experiencing the touch of moving limbs on her legs. Yes, she was sure of it. This was not a dream.

She instinctively picked up her phone, and though Sadie wasn't convinced that she could trust her mother at that moment, there was no one else to call.

"Mom?" she muttered.

Over her car's speakers, Morgan could hear soft puffs of irregular breath come through despite Sadie's efforts to conceal her agony. Before panic could set in, Morgan reminded herself to put on the most valiant mom-calming voice possible.

"Hey, honey, what's wrong?" she asked.

"Um, I... I was looking for that paperwork. And I..." Sadie drifted into silence as tears bubbled to the surface of her eyes.

"Sweetie?" Morgan probed. "What do you mean? Did something happen?" Morgan wrestled with the urge to leap into a frenzy.

"*You* know," Sadie replied as if challenging her mother to figure it out on her own so she wouldn't have to explain herself.

"Remember? I was asking you about my birth certificate. I need a passport. I talked with Emily earlier and I was telling her about the trip. I kind of complained that I still don't have it. She told me anything I needed should be in the office with some other paperwork. The blue lockbox Dad keeps his stuff in?" Sadie paused again to see if Morgan would investigate.

When she didn't, Sadie continued.

"So I went to look for my personal info file and..."

Sadie couldn't stifle her sobs any longer. She let out a guttural cry, unlike anything Morgan had heard from her daughter.

In a hurried panic, Morgan blurted, "I'm coming. Only ten minutes away, okay?"

She clicked the end call button on her car's screen and screamed.

"What the actual *hell*, Emily?!"

It wasn't often that Morgan's children spoke with their paternal grandmother, but somehow, her mother-in-law had positioned herself as the person in the twins' lives who could be relied on to answer a call and offer a solution at any given moment. It made Morgan see red. It was one of the things between them that they pretended didn't happen. They were good at ignoring the many ways they annoyed each other, smiling as if there had never been two more harmonious women on the planet. But for a couple of years, Morgan and Emily Connor had both been letting the mask slip.

Picking up speed, Morgan swerved her way through traffic and made it through the front door in under seven minutes.

"Sadie? Sadie!" Morgan shouted through the house until she entered the back office. Since she and Jarvis had bought the perfect, nearly six-thousand-square-foot home to raise their ideal family in, Jarvis had rarely used it for anything more than sipping an evening whiskey, collecting books, and keeping important records.

Morgan looked over at Sadie curled up in a ball, her back resting against the desk, arms wrapped around her legs, holding her knees close to her chest as she rocked slightly back and forth. Sadie heard her mother walk in but was entirely unmotivated to look up. She simply raised a birth certificate with the name Sadie Jane Connor above her head.

"That's why we call her Emily, isn't it? No *grandma* for her, nope. She's certainly too young for such a name. And what kind of excuse is that anyway? What other grandmother in the entire country insists that their grandkids call them by their first name, huh?"

Sadie resentfully lifted her head. The eyeliner Morgan and Jarvis had hesitantly allowed her to wear earlier that same year, making her look far older than her parents preferred, streaked Sadie's silky face.

"What are you talking about, baby?" Morgan wasn't being insincere. She truly hadn't put it together quite yet. She took a seat in front of her daughter, crossed her legs, and leaned her elbows onto her knees. All she wanted to do was be close enough to soothe her daughter's aching soul.

"It all makes sense now, Mom," Sadie said, meeting Morgan's eyes. "The way they treat us. Like we're the *other* family even though you and Dad have been married longer than any of the other aunts and uncles. I mean, I get it. They act like they have a just cause to mistreat you because they're condemning the whole sex-before-marriage thing."

Morgan blushed at the declaration, looking at Sadie with a raised eyebrow.

"Mom, c'mon. I figured out that you must have been pregnant when you guys got married by the time I was nine. But he's not even our *real Dad?* Why wouldn't you tell us that?"

Sadie put her hands in her lap again, as if she was going to cradle the paper with care, but instead let them rest on top of her knees as she sat simply staring at the information in black and white.

Without lifting her gaze, she began to hurl weighty questions that seemed to travel from her mouth to the floor, tumbling in slow motion as if each one was a crushing boulder.

"Is that why you put up with him? Because he holds it over you? He's the good guy who took in your bastard children, right?"

It was jarring for Morgan to hear not only the words but also the disdain that began to audibly rise within her only daughter.

"Sadie, please. You don't know what you're talking about."

"Oh, don't try to shush me, Mom. I'm not gonna let your dirty little secret get out."

"Sadie! Don't-" Morgan tried to continue, to stop Sadie from digging a hole she might soon regret, but Sadie kept going, causing Morgan to start processing the full extent of Sadie's knowledge.

"I mean, you could have at least put his name on the birth certificate, Mom. If you were going to give us his last name, you should've at least done that."

Sadie paused, letting a tear escape. It toppled down her cheek while Morgan stayed silent.

"*Unknown* is pretty stupid to write in the 'father' box if you ask me. Like, if you're going to live a lie, at least cover all your bases."

"Sadie, seriously. I'm telling you, you don't know what you're talking about."

"Don't I? Doesn't this prove that I'm right?" She took the document in her hands again, flapping it in front of her face as if to fan herself.

Morgan sighed. "It's one piece to a pretty complicated story. This didn't seem like something I could just bring up, and when I wanted to, your Dad didn't... But I never intended to hurt you. I wasn't willing to risk making you feel like you were unwanted."

"Not by you, no." Sadie wiped her tears and stood to her feet while slapping her birth certificate onto the large oak desk.

"Sadie, please." Morgan jumped up, grabbing her arm as Sadie quickly jerked her shoulder back.

"What? Please what? What can you possibly say to me to make this okay?"

"You're right. Nothing," Morgan whispered.

"Nothing I can say will ever make it okay that I haven't been fully honest with you. Every time the thought of telling you the truth came to my mind, I pushed it away, trying to justify the fact that you might not be old enough to handle it. I was wrong. I didn't know how to do it. And I'm sorry."

Sadie was stunned, unsure of how to receive her mother's confession. They both stood facing each other, trying to be strong for the other. Tears filled their eyes as sorrow and regret permeated the hollow gap between them. Sadie shook her head, finally breaking the silence.

"What are we gonna tell Milo?" she cried as she took a step forward, collapsing into her mother's arms, sobbing.

"Maybe I should tell you the whole story first?"

Morgan buckled with the weight of her daughter in her arms as she slid downward, her body gliding to the floor as she folded herself around the flesh of her child. She stroked her baby girl's hair, trying to see her as more than an infant, a toddler, a flailing dependent who couldn't do anything for herself.

Viewing your children's maturity as it truly is can be one of the hardest things to do as a mother, and Morgan knew she wasn't particularly skilled at it. Being raised by a mom who always treated her as if she was supposed to act like a grown-up, Morgan was determined to never force her children into maturity more quickly than she thought necessary. But even that approach came with its downfalls. Seeing her kids grow up faster than she was comfortable with came as a surprise she wasn't quite prepared for.

"Yeah, I think the whole story would be good, Mom. I think I'm ready," Sadie sighed.

"I would say so," Morgan tenderly assured her. "It's kind of a long story," she said, trying to figure out where to begin.

Sadie sat up from her mom's lap, scooting herself to the side. She rested her back against the long, wooden doors of the built-in bookshelves.

"I guess we've got nothing but time. Dad's at the warehouse and Milo's swim meet is today. Wait," Sadie said as if she just realized that her mom had rushed home to find her in a crumpled mess. "Did you leave him at the pool?"

"No, I dropped him off at the gym. The meet hasn't started yet. He's riding the bus over with the team. I told him I'd go to the pool and take him home from there if he wanted. Besides, I don't feel like sitting there for three hours waiting for his events while the *entire* gossip train whispers around me."

Sadie huffed. "Seriously. But you're not going to go and watch at all? Have you missed even one swim meet, like, ever?"

It was true she had not, and it hadn't gone unnoticed by her children. From the time the twins started music lessons and sports, no matter which instrument or what team they were playing on, Morgan hadn't missed a recital, play, game, or meet.

"Probably not," Morgan shrugged. That was a bit of false modesty. She knew full well she had never missed a moment. But this was a circumstance she couldn't ignore. Both of her children were simultaneously in need of support, yet she was only one person, split between two children, a fact that striated her heart.

"I'm sorry all this is happening, Mom," Sadie comforted, feeling the heaviness her mom was bearing.

"Me too, babe." Morgan sucked in a deep breath, smiling compassionately toward Sadie, letting the air slowly release again from her nostrils.

"But I am really mad at you, you know," Sadie continued. "I just can't seem to stay mad right now. It's a lot."

Morgan grinned at her sweet, sensitive, gloriously complicated daughter, feeling ever so lucky she was her mother. It was a strange sentiment. One she hadn't fully reconciled herself to, no matter how much therapy she had been in. She was grateful for her children. She was grateful for their lives. But did that make her grateful for the man who impregnated her? She couldn't know and allowed herself to be okay with the thought that she may never understand how being both thankful for her children and hating the man who gave them to her could live in the same space.

"What are we gonna do?"

Milo slipped his gym bag under the bed and gave it a swift kick. After dumping the contents on top of the bedspread, he began sorting his things methodically.

He wasn't like Sadie. Art, music, clothes, and anything she was interested in would eventually line the surface of her bedroom floor. Milo was precise, driven, and athletic. When presented with the facts, his reaction was completely rational. He was not entirely devoid of emotion, but to him, feelings were always secondary. Milo quickly moved from information-gathering straight into problem-solving mode. And Sadie was counting on it.

"*We,*" Sadie began as if she was introducing an object lesson, "are gonna find him," she announced excitedly, plopping herself onto the bed as she grabbed a throw pillow, hugging it closely.

"No way," Milo protested, yanking the pillow from her hand and placing it back in its rightful spot behind her. "Do you really want to do that?"

"Yeah, don't you?" Sadie snatched the pillow once again as she rested her back on the larger cushions along the headboard. Milo busied himself in his characteristic shuffle around the room, keeping it orderly.

"I don't know. I meant 'What are we gonna do about Dad?' Not 'What are we going to do about some sperm donor?'" Milo clarified.

"Oh, nice, Milo."

"What?" He turned to see Sadie contentedly nestled in. "And seriously? You're messing up the whole bed," he scolded, rolling his eyes.

Milo never did anything more than complain about Sadie disturbing his orderliness. He was used to his sister coming into his space for carefree late-night chats, clandestine iPad movie nights, and even early-morning secret-sharing sessions. Though he seemed to constantly oppose her invasions, he was all talk. Milo secretly loved having Sadie's precocious energy around him. He was like an older brother, acting the part of a more mature sibling. He simply followed his sister's trail of chaos, tidying the wreckage as they went along.

Milo continued to move around the room, placing his still-damp shorts over the hamper to dry, adjusting his shoes to make room for the ones he had taken off, and continuing his ritual of finding a proper place for everything.

"That's *exactly* what the guy is," he continued. "And what's the point of trying to find him? Dad has been a jackass lately, sure. But he's the one who has provided for us our whole lives. Even though he has a funny way of showing it sometimes, he's loved us in his own way."

Sadie unfolded her legs and stood, staring at her twin brother wide-eyed. She understood her mother better at that moment. She had told Milo some of the story. *Most* of the story. That their mom was already pregnant with them when their parents got married—something they hadn't discussed before, and Milo let her know that he had figured it out years prior as well. Then she told him that their dad wasn't the guy who got their mom pregnant. But she, too, had left out certain facts because Sadie wanted to spare Milo's feelings. And even though she knew he'd be reasonable about the information, she didn't expect to see him as almost robotic.

Milo shrugged and threw his hands in the air.

"What? What do you expect me to say? Poor us? We're so unfortunate that Mom didn't stay with the guy who knocked her up?"

Sadie couldn't let him go on without stopping his train of thought. She didn't want to hear what he might say next. She now realized it wasn't fair that she knew details he didn't.

"Milo, stop! She doesn't even know his *name!*"

Milo halted midstep, turning to look his sister in the eye as Sadie sunk back into the bed.

"And you're mad at *Dad?* Mom isn't innocent in all this, Sadie. Maybe things make more sense now."

Sadie wasn't sure if Milo thought things made sense because, according to the town rumor mill, their mom was a cheater and no one should be surprised since Morgan had a history of sexual promiscuity, or if Milo was simply connecting the dots of why they always felt like black sheep with the Connor side of the family. She immediately went into defense mode.

"No, you don't get it." Sadie wasn't screaming or arguing with any kind of intensity. Her energy seemed to be drained as she uttered the words after taking a long breath. "Mom was raped."

Milo stopped and stared at his sister, then plopped himself next to her with a sigh.

After a long pause, he nudged his sister and said, "Um, you could have led with that!"

"What was I supposed to say? Mom was raped and that's why we're here?" Sadie's voice was full of pity for her brother. It was as if she'd forgotten that they shared the same story.

"Yeah. Kind of," he said.

"But that's pretty intense."

"Yeah," Milo spoke in a whispered staccato. "Yeah."

The twins sat in silence for a few moments, resting their backs on the enormous fluffy pile Milo was currently unbothered about crumpling. They sat quietly motionless until the stillness broke with the buzz of Sadie's phone. She picked it up to see an Instagram notification.

"Oh my gosh, seriously?"

Sadie tilted her screen toward Milo.

"Ugh, another one?" Milo groaned.

"Yeah. I dare you to block him," Sadie smirked.

"Dude. *You* block him."

They lingered on the bed as Sadie rested her head on Milo's shoulder. Though she had sprouted taller and faster than her twin brother for the first ten years of their lives, Milo had grown into his own body and finally looked like he could be the same age or even older. It was as if Sadie at long last had a big brother, something she was often jealous of when her girlfriends had kind and caring older siblings. Milo had counted on Sadie for most of their childhood, but at this stage, the roles were reversing, and they both settled into them willingly.

"You know something?" Milo's voice sliced through the silence once again.

"What?"

"Our parents suck," he chuckled.

Sadie smiled and nodded.

"Yeah, but don't they look *so great* on social media?" she said in her best impression of a hustling boss-babe voice.

Since the spray paint incident, and his children's refusal to speak to him directly other than to answer yes and no questions, Jarvis had been sharing mental health quotes on Instagram in a series he liked to call "to my children." His captions, full of cliches and reductive tropes, were replete with run-on sentences of advice to his kids, particularly naming what he found problematic about the world at large. One could assume there was an underlying message. Either Jarvis had the best parenting style in the world, with amazing children who had the greatest personalities on the planet, or his kids were complete terrors and he thought public admonition might be an effective tool.

The jury of social media would remain relatively split.

Sadie rushed into Milo's room waving her phone around.

"I got it. I mean, I *think* I have something."

She was practically out of breath as she clutched the device close to her chest.

"What? What is it?" Milo removed an earbud from his right ear, looking at her with a puzzled expression. "You're holding a phone, Sadie."

Milo raised an eyebrow in his typical, nothing-is-that-urgent way. He had learned not to take his sister too seriously since her approach to life was nothing if not exaggeratedly spirited. Sadie's exuberance didn't generate excitement in him very often. Milo had repeatedly fallen prey to his sister's crying wolf routine, a habit in their early years. During their adolescence, he decided to remain nonchalant about most things for his sanity.

"Milo, I got the email," she said, once again waving the phone around. "The one that will tell me, well, *may* tell me, erm, us... Milo, this might be the answer about who he is."

Milo's eyes widened as he froze in place. He intentionally narrowed his gaze, placing his phone down on the bed next to him and removing the other earbud from his ear.

"What are you talking about?" Milo thought he knew exactly what his twin sister was up to. If he was right, he was going to make her say it. "What did you do, Sadie?"

"Well, remember I told you I ordered that kit?"

"Yeah, and?"

"I sent it in," she admitted excitedly, albeit suddenly filled with a sense of guilt for going against her brother's advice.

"C'mon, Sadie. You're probably supposed to be eighteen on those sites for a reason. You know you could get busted, right? Did you even use your real name?"

"Um, no," she said flippantly. "I'm not stupid." Sadie could hardly believe Milo would insinuate that she'd make that kind of error.

"Geez. Let me see it." Milo stood up from the bed and reached his hand toward his sister, gesturing for her to hand him the phone.

"So, you're not mad?" Sadie asked enthusiastically,

"What use is it to either of us if I say I'm mad?" Milo shrugged.

Sadie smiled at her brother, bouncing nervously toward him with a giggle, and stretched herself upward, reaching his cheek to give him a tiny kiss.

"Thanks for not being mad. Should I grab my laptop so we can look at it together?"

"Sure," Milo replied in his typical monosyllabic manner. It wasn't that he didn't have emotion, he was just really good at not expressing it. He was, in fact, elated. The slight upward curl of his lip was the only indication. He loved Sadie and was more than curious to know about their origin. But he convinced himself that he was fine either way. This wouldn't change a thing.

As Milo sat on the edge of the bed, Sadie reentered from the shared bathroom that connected their bedrooms. Milo had begged and pleaded to move into the basement room. Instead, Jarvis had remodeled it for his wine collection. It was now a seating and tasting area rather than a bedroom. Milo had argued that his sister could finally have all the girl time she needed in a bathroom that, in his mind, no longer made sense for them to share. He wasn't interested in overtaking the guest room with access to a hallway bathroom. He was the type of kid who was overly cautious, thinking he would be an imposition on his family if he requested too much.

"Okay, I'll have to sign in," Sadie said as she lowered herself to the bed. Her enthusiasm had begun to take on the tone of trepidation.

Milo put his hand on her knee. "Do you want to do this?" he asked his sister earnestly.

"Don't you?" she asked.

"Yeah, I guess I do. But do you think there's a chance that the guy who got mom pregnant just happened to make a 23andme account?"

"He doesn't have to. People who are related to him could have made one. It's a whole network. There's, like, 10 million people on here," Sadie explained.

"Dude. Okay, let's do it," Milo agreed as he took a big gulp of air.

Sadie signed in as the two gazed at the screen, hopeful, scared, enthralled, and terrified. She clicked the tab titled "Your results." Regions of the US, Europe, South America, and North Africa were illuminated. As children, they heard many stories of how their family arrived in the States, married among the tribes, the settlers, and everything in between, but it was confusing to see it in digital form.

"Interesting," Milo blurted, "but how do we know if there are relatives?"

"Here," Sadie clicked another tab.

As the siblings watched the computer screen, neither one of them uttered a sound as they scrolled and clicked through tabs and pages. Sadies fingers came to a stop when she saw they did, indeed, have relatives who were registered on the platform. Faces they recognized. People they *knew*.

"I don't get it. Aunt Clarice is related to us? But if Dad isn't our *biological* dad, how is that possible?" Milo looked at Sadie, unable to process what he was seeing. "Is this some sick joke?"

"No, I don't understand either. I mean, it says *unknown* in the dad section of our birth certificates, Milo."

"But they were married when we were born," Milo said incredulously.

"Yeah. They were, right? How is that even a thing? Why would Dad refuse to put his name on our birth certificate?"

"Why would he do that?" Milo echoed, shaking his head. " It just doesn't make sense."

"None of this makes sense, Milo."

Sadie closed the laptop.

"Hey, hello? What's up, girl?" Tiffany answered cheerfully. She was always delighted to see her pseudo-niece's face fill her phone's screen. She greeted her in the same chipper voice every time.

"Aunt Tiffany?" Sadie hesitated. "Um, what time do you get off work?"

"I'm not working, babe."

"Oh, good," Sadie sighed.

"What's going on, Sadie? Are you all right? Is it your mom?"

Tiffany uncharacteristically jumped to impossible scenarios in her mind after hearing the distress in Sadie's voice. Morgan had told her about Sadie finding the birth certificate and how she relayed the whole truth about the twins, their father, and Morgan's pregnancy. Though Tiffany thought it was long overdue, everything in their lives seemed volatile. It was enough to rattle even the strongest of friends.

Sadie continued. She wasn't crying. She was genuinely con-fused. "It's not Mom. It's me. Kind of. I just... I need to talk to you."

"Okay, wanna meet somewhere?"

"No, I don't want this to be in public. Can I come over?" Sadie asked.

"Of course you can. But do you need a ride?"

"No. I'll take my bike. I'll see you in a bit, okay?"

CHAPTER 6
ESCAPE

S ADIE RODE HER BIKE to a thin walkway around a large
building on a street lined with apartments and duplexes.
She popped the wheels up onto the curb and stepped on
top of the old concrete. Some of the homes on Walton Way
were larger than others, housing quaint one-bedroom apartments with four or six units a piece, but Tiffany's was one of
the smaller buildings with airy three-bedroom open-concept
units, two total, one stacked atop the other. Proud and meticulous about home ownership, Tiffany had bought the building years earlier and had a steady flow of students from the
medical school rent the bottom floor while she lived above.
Sadie loved the university housing streets with its energetic
vibe. To her, it made complete sense that her Aunt Tiffany
lived here.

Sadie punched the numbers to the code for the side door
entrance, pulled her bike into the hallway, and set it against
the wall. Just as she was about to walk up the stairs, her phone
buzzed. Removing it from her pocket, she saw the screen

illuminate with a picture of her and Tiffany making goofy faces. She laughed under her breath. Sadie wasn't used to seeing the photo come up on her phone since she was in the habit of texting, and it was enough to give her a little comfort, knowing she'd reached out to the right person. She slid her finger across the screen and lifted the phone to her ear.

"Hey, Aunt Tiffany. I'm here."

"Okay, cool. I wondered if you'd get there before I did. I'm just pulling up now. I was at the grocery store when you called."

"Oh, man. I'm so sorry-"

Tiffany cut her off.

"No, no. It's fine. I'm just grabbing the ice cream from my car and coming in now."

Sadie put her phone back into her pocket, turned towards the door again, opened it wide, and saw Tiffany carrying a bit more than ice cream.

"I just grabbed the refrigerator bags." Tiffany shrugged, walking briskly toward Sadie. "Thanks," she continued as she squeezed herself through the door.

The two walked up the stairs and inside the apartment without saying anything else, Sadie taking a bag to relieve some of the effort from her aunt before they went up. As they entered, both went straight to the kitchen, busily putting items in the fridge and freezer, still without an utterance.

When the food was all in its rightful places, Tiffany laid her reusable, strawberry-patterned shopping bag on the kitchen island, leaned her elbows on the marble, and finally spoke.

"So, you called me."

"Yeah," Sadie replied with a sigh.

"What's up, love?"

Sadie took her phone from her pocket, opened the 23andme app, and slid it across the crisp countertop.

"What am I looking at here?"

"I... Um... I took a DNA test," Sadie admitted.

Soft creases formed across Tiffany's forehead as she lifted her eyebrows, tilting her head to the side.

"Oh, babe. Okay," Tiffany hesitated, placing the phone face down on the counter without looking further. "So," she paused, "I haven't talked to you since your mom explained things, right?"

"No," Sadie said impatiently. "But now... Only Milo knows that I did this. And I don't know who else to talk to. I just don't understand."

"Okay, I can imagine. But, is there anything you want to ask me before we talk about what's on this app?" Tiffany cautioned herself, tamping her desire to go into a full-blown lecture.

"I think you should see it first," Sadie replied.

"Fair enough." Tiffany picked up the phone again, cradling it in her left hand and navigating the screen with her right. She let out a sigh. "Let's take a look."

She tapped and swiped the screen slowly. Her expression was hard to read at first, but Sadie watched her eyes widen, taking in the shocking information Sadie was unwilling to process alone.

"Wait. Can I ask you something?" Tiffany spoke cautiously.

"Yeah, of course."

"What did your mom tell you about what happened?"

Sadie scoffed. "You know you don't have to check my mom's facts against yours. You can tell me the truth. I'm almost 16 years old."

Tiffany grinned. "Babe, I'm just trying to put the pieces together myself, okay? I wasn't with her that night, and I only know what she told me. I'm not gonna break her trust and give you details that aren't easy to deal with, you know?"

Sadie wasn't often frustrated with her Aunt Tiffany, but at that moment she started to wonder if she'd made a mistake by going there.

"Are you serious? *Hard to deal with?* Of course it's hard to deal with. Every detail of this situation is hard to deal with!"

"I don't mean to upset you, Sadie. I'm trying to figure this out too." Tiffany shifted to the other side of the kitchen island, putting her hand on Sadie's arm. "I want what's best for you, sweetie. You know that."

Sadie's eyes softened from anger to despair. She did know. A warm tear began to bead at the corner of her eye before it swelled, popping off her thick eyelashes and careening onto her right cheek.

"Yeah. I know."

Sadie quickened the rhythm of her words, hoping to speed up the process of just getting to the point.

"Mom told me she didn't remember a lot about that night other than she was at a party and was raped. She didn't know who did it or if it was more than one guy because there were a lot of people there kissing and stuff before she blacked out. She said she felt drugged, but it could have been that she was just drinking a lot."

"Oh, she was drugged. I don't think there's a question about that," Tiffany interjected.

"So then how is this possible?" Sadie hesitated. "I mean, you're reading what I'm reading, right?"

Tiffany reached for the phone again to look at the DNA relatives tab.

"Yeah, that's what it says," Tiffany confirmed, taking a slow breath inward.

"So make it make sense to me," Sadie pleaded.

Tiffany calmly lowered the phone to the countertop, the screen facing downward. She let the air she'd be holding in her lungs expel with a quick sigh.

"Sadie, there's only one explanation. Maybe we should sit down."

The two walked toward the couch as if tiptoeing across a slick patch of ice. Slowly, silently, hand in hand. As they lowered themselves to the seats, another tear trickled down Sadie's face.

"Did she tell you he was there?" Tiffany asked.

"What do you mean? My dad? Like, at the party?"

"Yeah. That's why I wanted you to tell me what your mom said. I wasn't sure if you knew. It's kind of how your parents got together."

"Hold on," Sadie shook her head and spoke almost mockingly, "'*Kind of how they got together?*' She was embarrassed that they slept together at a party, so she made up a bizarre story about why my dad's name isn't on my birth certificate?"

Sadie rose to her feet, feeling a tight constriction in her lungs as if she was about to be completely out of breath. Panic washed over her, and the air she sucked in couldn't fully get past her throat. She clasped her hands to her heart as if it was about to burst. The word heartbreaking wasn't an expression. It was motion, a movement, an ailment that had no cure.

Tiffany stood, calmly taking Sadie's hands into hers, and mindfully lowered both herself and Sadie back onto the couch.

"Breathe. It's okay. Just take a minute," she instructed.

Tiffany stroked her young niece's back just as she had done when she and Sadie's mother were that age. She couldn't help but release a few soft cries herself. She deepened her breathing as the two finally sat quietly again, resting their backs on the sofa, shoulder to shoulder.

"Are you saying this whole thing was made up? You can tell me. I can handle it." Sadie finally spoke.

"No, that's not what I'm saying. Your mother doesn't have any idea that it could be him. I never would have imagined it myself. What I meant was, Jarvis... Erm, your dad called her the next day. Checking in, you know? He told her that he hadn't seen her after a certain point during the party and that he just wanted to make sure she was okay. And that's kind of, well, how they started dating."

Sadie spoke through a few last broken breaths. "Okay... So you're saying that the only explanation is that my father is my mother's rapist. That *is* what you're saying right? And she doesn't know it?"

In an instant, the weight of the world seemed to collapse upon Sadie's shoulders, as if the walls of the room were closing in, suffocating her with the enormity of the news. Shock washed over her like an icy wave, numbing her senses and leaving her paralyzed in disbelief as time slowed to a crawl, each heartbeat echoing loudly in the silent room.

Tiffany's breath caught in her throat, unable to escape the crushing grip of reality. She was finding it difficult to admit to herself, much less to one of her favorite people on the planet, that they'd all been calculatedly deceived the entire time.

Every sound became distant, muffled by the overwhelming rush of emotions flooding both of their minds. At that moment, the two women felt small and insignificant, adrift in a sea of turmoil, grappling with the harsh truth that had shattered their world.

Minutes felt like hours, their minds racing with unanswered questions and unspoken emotions. Then, suddenly, as if breaking through a barrier of uncertainty, Sadie's voice shattered the silence. "I should go," she said.

"No, please don't," Tiffany begged, shaking her head not only in protest but to rattle her mind back from its reeling thoughts and into the present moment.

"Aunt Tiffany, if Mom doesn't know…If Dad was so determined for her never to find out he was her rapist that he was willing to exclude his name from his own children's birth certificates, ashamed of what it would mean, then this changes nothing. We can't…We can't do anything, can we?"

Tiffany put her hand on Sadie's knee.

"I think it had more to do with inheritance than with your dad being ashamed. I know he loves you both. In his own way..."

"Oh, stop. Why does everyone give him a pass? '*In his own way?*' What does that even mean? And why do people keep saying it?"

Sadie froze, realizing what Tiffany had just admitted. She locked eyes with her.

"Wait. Inheritance? You think Emily *knows?*"

"No. Sadie..." Tiffany was simply processing aloud, immediately full of regret that she had verbalized anything.

Sadie didn't break her stare, though. Tiffany squirmed, looking down at her lap, trying to catalog years of circumstances, lies, truths, and her own memories within milliseconds.

"I just think that Emily knows the same story we all do. Jarvis had to have told her the 'unknown rapist' version of events. I mean, if there's anyone on the planet that man seeks to impress at all costs it's his mother. She wouldn't have accepted you and Milo, your mom, *or* your dad if she knew the truth. Had the Connors known he got a girl pregnant in college, they would have dismissed him from his seat on his family firm's board of directors and made up some story about how he took his own path without a blink. No, they *have* to know the story of him being the rescuer," Tiffany proceeded convincingly. "They're too proud to embrace their oldest son over their principles. And that would have killed him."

Tiffany paused, trying to sort information before she continued.

"No, I think that Emily consented to the marriage knowing your mom was pregnant, thinking it was someone else's baby, and made your dad promise he could play the hero, keep their secret, but agree to not put his name on your birth certificates. That way, no assets would be passed down to non-blood relatives. They are weird about that down there. It's like a *cult,* that family."

Regret cascaded over her once again as Tiffany clasped a hand to her mouth.

Sadie sat in stunned silence as the words sank in. She had always imagined her future with a sense of security, knowing that her grandparents' wealth would cushion any fall. But now, as the reality hit her, she felt a profound sense of loss and uncertainty. For years, she had taken comfort in the thought that her grandparents' legacy would provide stability, yet now she faced the daunting prospect of forging her path without the safety net she had relied on. It wasn't just about the money; it was about the sense of belonging and security that seemed to vanish in an instant.

As Sadie grappled with this revelation, she realized that her journey toward self-reliance and independence had just taken an unexpected turn, one that would test her resilience and strength in ways she had never imagined. The two sat in temporary limbo before Sadie rubbed her knees, ultimately slapping her hands against them.

"It's okay. I needed the truth today," Sadie said determinedly.

"I guess the redeeming truth here is that your dad's shame gave him some sense of duty not to abandon you entirely," Tiffany encouraged.

"Sorry if I can't agree with you there," Sadie sneered.

Anguish mingled with fury, forming a tempest within her soul as she struggled to reconcile the duality of a man who was both her father and the perpetrator of unspeakable harm. Yet, amidst the tumult of emotions, one thing remained clear—Sadie would not allow his actions to go unchallenged, for her mother's sake and her own.

"It would have been better if he had left us all alone from the start," she spouted. "Because I wouldn't have a broken mother."

Sadie's tears had vanished—turned into acrimony—as she began to steel herself for anything. She knew she'd have to be strong when she told Milo. That was her priority. Then, she'd wash her hands of it all. But there *was* one thing.

"I don't think Mom can know. Not now. It's too much," she said firmly.

Tiffany immediately began shaking her head in protest.

"Sadie, listen. You have to understand. This is the only, solitary thing that she *absolutely* deserves to know. It explains every detail we've wondered about for years. It's not fair that your mom blames herself for any little part of her life that isn't impossibly perfect. But it's another thing that your dad blames her. We *have* to tell her," Tiffany insisted. "She deserves that."

Sadie stood, moving toward the door.

"*We* don't have to do anything. If you want to tell her, that's your business. But if it breaks her, I'll hold you responsible. Forever," she said harshly.

"Sadie, wait. What are you going to do?"

"*Do?* I'm going to live my life avoiding both of my parents until my dad kicks my mom out of the house or she finally finds the strength to leave him. Whichever comes first."

Sadie threw her hands in the air.

"And when I'm old enough, I'm going to leave this place and never look back."

Morgan watched tiny bubbles of golden champagne filter to the top of her glass and then pop open in miniature bursts on its surface. She was transfixed. It wasn't uncommon for her to enjoy a chilled glass on the weekends, relaxing in a plush chair on the back veranda, but since *the incident*, she hadn't offered herself the pleasure. Until today.

She sat with her legs pulled to her chest, her back resting against the side of the wide chair and her toes pressing against the opposite section. When Jarvis opened the wide French doors to step outside, she didn't even bother breaking her gaze from the champagne flute.

"Oh, I didn't expect to see you out here," Jarvis said. He moved slowly toward her, scotch in hand, and lowered himself warily onto the seat across from her.

Morgan lifted the glass to her lips, taking a soft sip, allowing the bubbles to caress her nose. She grinned.

"What's up with you?" Jarvis asked hesitantly.

"Me?" Morgan snorted.

"Yeah, you're acting weird."

Morgan chuckled under her breath. "Acting weird," she smirked.

"Yeah, like that. I mean, you've been holed up in your room all this time, not saying much of anything night or day, and now you're sitting on the back porch, smiling and sipping champagne, not bothering to get up or even look at me?"

Morgan shot her eyes toward him as her head tilted just enough to allow him to know she was purposely directing her unbroken gaze on him as she lifted the glass to her lips again, taking in a leisurely, audible slurp.

"Are you drunk?" Jarvis scrutinized.

"Not likely. This is my first." Morgan swished the glass in front of her nose.

"Okay... Well, I guess it's good that you're over your phase of playing the victim then."

"What does that even mean?" Morgan insisted. "That's so stupid. People say don't *play the victim,* don't *act* the victim, don't *be* a victim. But when you're victimized, then what? It's a label you're not supposed to wear? So stupid."

"Oh, c'mon. Do you think I victimized you? Get over yourself, Morgan."

"Should I? Really? *Get over myself?*" she mocked. "I mean, you went into a rage and defaced our property, Jarvis." She waved her finger in front of her chest. "I didn't do that."

"Oh, okay," he scoffed. "I victimized private property that I paid for myself. Sure. Guilty. I don't think that's a chargeable offense."

"You posted pictures on the internet, Jay. I had to permanently delete my Instagram *and* Facebook. I've had those accounts for so long."

"You could've made them private," Jarvis pointed out. "Blocked people. Don't blame me for that."

"Yeah, I could've. And I did before I deleted them. But again, how is this my responsibility when I wasn't the one who lost their mind?"

"No? Really? Go cry to your boyfriend." Jarvis crossed one leg over the other to indicate he was going nowhere and would not be backing down anytime soon. "Then we'll see who's guilty of what."

"Oh, cool. You get to declare whatever you want to the world. Sure." Morgan took another sip. "Because being on the internet is verifiable evidence of the cheating wife, right?"

"Are you denying it? Saying you don't have a boyfriend? I mean, that'd be ironic, because I'm pretty sure the church elders are meeting tonight to vote on whether or not to fire him. Precisely because it *is* true."

Morgan shot her eyes at Jarvis.

"What? They're firing Johnny?" she asked in shock.

"I would think so. It's only appropriate."

"Says who?" Morgan demanded. "The people who never bothered to call or talk to me about any of it? No, it's fine to be talked about rather than spoken to." She slammed back the last sip of champagne. "Bastards."

"Spoken like an innocent victim," Jarvis jeered.

"Ha. It's all good." Morgan flung her head back, rolling her eyes. "I know exactly who is guilty, and probably for the very first time in my life." She shook her head excessively. "Yeah, that's right, Jarvis. I know exactly who is guilty," she repeated as she pointed her finger in the air toward him.

Morgan lowered the glass to the table as she slung her feet to the ground, turning to the champagne stand on her left, pulling the bottle from the ice, and revealing that more than one glass had been poured.

"Well, look at that. Perhaps I am a little tipsy. But thinking clear as day, Jarvis Connor. Clear. As. Day."

"I don't know what has gotten into you or what you think you're doing, Morgan, but trust me, you don't want to go there with me," Jarvis said as he leaned toward her, narrowing his eyes.

"Oh, you're right about that," she laughed. "I don't want to go anywhere with you at all. And I'm staying put until I absolutely feel like it."

Jarvis let out a sinister guffaw. "What does that mean? You're threatening to sit there? Cool. Not to make me dinner? Fine. Don't be petty, Morgan. I can outlast you."

He shot his scotch to the back of his throat as he stood up to leave. Morgan considered even that a small victory. She wasn't going to run away in fear. If he wanted to be left alone, then he could leave. But she didn't quite feel finished. Whether it was the liquid courage she had been sipping on all afternoon or that she finally arrived at her breaking point, she knew she was ready.

"Why didn't you just ask for a divorce instead of humiliating me?" she called out as Jarvis walked toward the door. "You of all people know I never slept with anyone. Since you have trackers on me and everything."

Jarvis stopped, midstep, and turned to look at her.

"Divorce? You're saying you want a divorce, Morgan?"

"I'm asking why you hate me so much," Morgan said, sounding completely sober for the first time during their exchange. "And why you would have to spy on someone you said you love."

Jarvis smirked.

"You don't know anything."

"Oh, but I do. You were right about something. I do have a friend. Not one whose bed I've jumped into, but one who has helped me figure some things out. Tech, in particular. You know, uninstall things on my phone. Set up some rerouting stuff."

She took her phone from her pocket, shaking it back and forth.

Jarvis inched closer to her, giving her an all-too-familiar look. He spoke forcefully, rhythmically. "Don't push me, Morgan. You ain't seen nothin' yet."

She steadied her focus on him, casting her steely gaze from the phone she held in her hands to lock eyes with the man she had cowered to for years. Something in her had snapped, like a rubber band that was stretched so thin it had nothing left in it but a vicious bounce.

Jarvis glared at her as if attempting to bore his stare into her flesh. It had worked in the past, making the impalpable intent of his spiteful accusations all too real on Morgan's skin. But today, she deflected the fiery darts of his contempt.

He was the first to look away and that alone bolstered Morgan's resolve.

"I'm going inside," Jarvis finally spoke, turning toward the house again.

"So you're not interested in seeing what I found today? I mean, this app is pretty great," Morgan mocked.

"I'm not interested in anything you're saying or doing, Morgan."

Jarvis flicked his hand as if swatting away an annoying bug.

"Okay. I didn't think much of it. I haven't been paying close attention. You know, distracted as I've been wearing the scarlet, or should I say bright blue, letter *A* around town thanks to you."

"I can't hear you!" His singsong tone made Morgan's skin crawl.

"Well, hear this Jarvis. I have the DNA results. Sadie signed up for 23andMe. The app she installed conveniently downloaded on my phone thanks to that parental control software. So, I opened it," she explained, speaking loudly enough for him to hear, nearly shouting as he froze at the threshold between the terrace door and the stony cement.

Jarvis' face flushed as he swung himself around again to look in her direction. He threw the crystal glass with a force that would rival professional athletes. Morgan ducked her head as it whizzed past her, shattering to pieces on the ground.

"Dammit, Morgan. What have you done?"

Jarvis picked up a metal chair close to him and hurled it blindly, cracking two panes of thick glass segmented between the mullions on the heavy French doors. Scanning the area for another item, he yanked an oversized clay pot with its towering cedar still intact, splitting it against the masonry of the stairs that led to the lower level of the patio.

Morgan slipped her phone back into her pocket and crept sideways around the corner of the covered terrace. Cushioned sofas and chairs lined her escape as she crept her way to a side door. She entered quietly, moving herself briskly up the stairs, still able to hear distant sounds of items being fractured against walls and floors. She made a beeline to her bedroom, recovering an overnight bag, fully packed. She wasn't sure why she did it—packed a travel bag when she moved from the master into the guest room—but perhaps it was a premonition.

She ran up the stairs to check the twins' rooms. She knew Sadie had been at Tiffany's. She could check her phone and see when her kids were at any time. Milo was at Jake's house, working on a science project, but it must have been a mom thing. A magnetic pull had her running up there to double-check.

Finding their rooms empty, she breathed a sigh of relief and hurried to the ground floor again, attempting to be as soundless as possible. But there he stood. Right around the corner where she had set the bag before dashing up the steps to see if her children truly weren't inside the house.

"Going somewhere?" Jarvis said calmly.

"Yes."

Morgan swallowed hard. The truth was, Jarvis had never once laid a finger on her. He had thrown things before, sure. But a plate against the kitchen floor or a book across the room wasn't anything to get alarmed over, she told herself. Even society would back her up on it. He didn't hit you? It's not abuse. But this wasn't like before. She wasn't just afraid of his outburst. She felt a fear she had not yet known.

"I'm going to stay with Tiffany tonight," Morgan tried to make her voice sound stronger than a whisper. "You obviously need time to cool down."

"I'm fine. I just needed to blow off some steam," Jarvis replied coyly.

Morgan stood wide-eyed and motionless, unsure of how to respond to his apathetic tone.

"You should clean up this mess," Jarvis said, lifting Morgan's overnight bag to his chest and moving down the hallway, stepping over a broken vase, then eventually closing the massive oak door of his office.

Morgan blankly stared at the disorder. She allowed a tear to trickle down her cheek.

"Mom!" Sadie exclaimed as she approached. Morgan hadn't heard her enter the garage door just seconds earlier.

"Shhh..." Morgan heedfully lifted a finger to her mouth.

Barely uttering a sound, Morgan removed her index finger from her lips and pointed. Shaking her head from side to side, she motioned for Sadie to go upstairs without a word.

"What happened?" Sadie mouthed.

Morgan leaned into her daughter, pulling Sadie's ear to her mouth and whispering as softly as possible.

"Get what you can. We have to leave. Now."

Sadie tiptoed as fast as she could up the stairs as Morgan shuffled the broken glass and flowers around with her feet, trying to mimic the sounds of cleaning up, keeping a steady eye on the office door. Within moments, Sadie returned with one backpack in her arms.

"That's it?" Morgan muttered.

"I don't need anything else," Sadie responded as the two tried to communicate with as few words as possible.

Morgan hugged her daughter's arm to hers and led her out the front door and down the street. They picked up their pace, not quite running, but noticeably moving more quickly than they would when taking a leisurely neighborhood stroll.

"What do we do now?" Sadie asked as they cleared the houses on their side of the street and turned a corner.

"Text Milo. Tell him when he's done to meet us at the park, okay?"

"Okay, but..."

Morgan pulled her phone to her ear as Sadie heard her mother say, "Hey, Tiff. I need your help. Can you come to the park and pick us up?"

Once they got to the neighborhood entrance in view of the park, they settled into a steady jog. As they gained more and more distance, Morgan's phone buzzed.

"Your dad is moving. He must have come out of his office and noticed I'm not there," she said as she looked at her screen.

"You got a tracking app on *Dad?*" Sadie asked in a horrified tone.

"We'll talk about that later. Just run."

The most well-known mother-daughter duo in the neighborhood began to run towards the park, hoping to go unnoticed. They soon found a pavilion that had a long table with rows of benches around a large cement barbeque pit.

"We'll crouch down over there. He won't be able to see us behind those cinder blocks. I'll text Tiffany and Milo where to find us," Morgan instructed.

Dark skies descended, blanketing the atmosphere with a sharp coolness. Spring nights were playing tug-of-war with temperate days since the heavy rains had subsided, but every evening the chill fell fast. Morgan nuzzled herself close to Sadie as she buried her face into her mother's neck.

"Is that him?" Sadie whispered as they both hunched further, making themselves as small as possible, unable to see if Jarvis' car had been the one passing.

"I don't know. Tiffany should be here any second. If Milo doesn't get here soon too, I'm afraid your dad will see him."

"Well, check Milo's location," Sadie suggested.

"Oh, yeah, good point. I didn't get a notification that he's on the move, so maybe he's still at Jake's."

Morgan looked at her phone, swiped to find her app, and clicked on Milo's name.

"Whew, good. He *is* still there. I'll text him and tell him to stay put. Did he read your message already? Maybe he didn't even get it."

"Read my message?" Sadie reacted. "Mom, he doesn't have his *read-messages* thing on. That's gross."

"Gross, huh?" Morgan smiled.

"It's just weird. And when our parents track us, that's weird too." Sadie couldn't help but give her opinion. "Anyway, I'll just text him that we are coming to get him. He can leave his bike there tonight, I guess."

"Yeah, I'll text him too. Hopefully, he'll hear or see one of them soon. I don't want to freak him out when we show up at the Foleson's house."

"Well, it's Milo, Mom. He'll be fine," Sadie assured, knowing her brother would be bothered by the fact that his evening plans were overridden, but likely wouldn't react.

Another set of headlights extended over the tables and through the pavilion, coming closer, and then came to a stop at the parking spaces near the barbeque pit.

"Oh, sweet, it's Aunt Tiffany!" Sadie said as she popped her head over the concrete.

Morgan and Sadie ran to the car, rapidly piling themselves in and shutting the doors behind them without a word of explanation.

"Hey," Tiffany greeted briskly.

"Hey. You know where the Folesons live?" Sadie asked, leaning forward from behind the driver's seat, and keeping the need for explanations at a minimum.

"Yeah," Tiffany replied, needing no further information.

"Cool, let's get Milo."

They traveled the six-minute drive in silence. It was as if the moment they had all been waiting for had finally come and no one was sure how to handle it other than continuing to move. Words weren't needed.

As Tiffany pulled her car into the driveway, Morgan let out a long sigh.

"I'll need to tell them something," she hesitated.

"You're here to pick up your son," Tiffany assured her, nodding as she put one hand on top of Morgan's. "It's okay. You've got this."

CHAPTER 7
REPUTATION

JENNY FOLESON WALKED BACKSTAGE to the countertop spread of goodies and filled a small plate with fruit.

"Hey, Jenny!"

She heard a cheerful voice behind her as she shifted toward the coffee maker. A wave of irritation crashed against her chest. Her eyes closed slowly as she took in a deep breath. Despite Jenny's training on how to understand people, she struggled with some. This person in particular. She sensed that she could decipher the true meaning behind the chipper tone, but mentally admonished herself not to be too harsh. Second-guessing oneself is something even seasoned therapists do, and Jenny was no exception. She did her best to remain cordial.

"Oh, hey, Jarvis. Um, how are you?"

"Livin' the dream," Jarvis said as he picked up a donut in one hand and stood twirling a drumstick like a baton in the other. He shoved half of the sticky pastry into his mouth and looked at Jenny blankly as if waiting for her to say something.

Chuckling awkwardly, Jenny directed her attention to the creamers as she began to pour a bit of hazelnut-flavored almond milk into her cup, attempting to discourage any further dialogue.

"So, what's going on with you this morning? You're not your usual bubbly self," Jarvis said in a tone few others would assume was accusatory as he leaned against the counter and tapped the drumstick on the hard surface.

Jenny had been volunteering with Jarvis long enough to know that his comment was more than an observation. She didn't turn to look at him, not yet. All she could think was, *Why do you insist on carrying one drumstick with you as if no one knows what you do around here? Acting like you aren't the subject of everyone's gossip just because Morgan takes the brunt of it all. And it is* not *my responsibility to be bubbly. Jackass.*

But she didn't dare say it aloud. Turning to face him, she mustered the best smile she could.

"I'm just having a morning," she responded dryly.

"Well, snap out of it, woman. You're about to go onstage!"

Jenny bit her lip. *Did he just call me 'woman?'* "I'll be fine," she managed to say without sounding completely perturbed.

"Well, it's a must!" he chuckled.

Jarvis had a way of speaking with a smirk or a laugh that would make people question if he possessed the ability to be serious. Even though he'd talk about some pretty serious subjects while doing it. But since he approached practically everything in a lighthearted way, Jarvis would repeat demeaning and insulting comments and get away with it. Always.

"You're the best singer we've got," Jarvis continued as he moved closer, giving Jenny a little nudge on the shoulder. He tossed the last bit of the donut into his mouth, not bothering to finish chewing before saying, "And good for you stickin' to the fruit. Three miles this morning or I'd be doin' the same." He slapped his thighs as if congratulating his quads for the morning run.

Things like that. Everyone would tolerate Jarvis' comments because who's to say if he was admiring Jenny's self-control or drawing attention to the fact that he thought she should watch her weight? No one Jenny knew would ever call him out on it. Including herself.

Jarvis sauntered to the seating area in the expansive green room for Sunday morning performers, leaving Jenny standing alone at the coffee bar. She watched him walk away then looked at the plate of donut holes in front of her and stuffed one in her mouth just because. Consuming food with sugar and dairy wasn't the best decision for someone who had to be on the platform to lead a few thousand people in worship songs in less than ten minutes, but it sure felt good going down.

"Babe, I've been thinking about the Connors," Jenny said as she and her husband cleaned up dishes from their Sunday lunch with the kids.

The Foleson clan was the type of family people portrayed in movies. Not that they put on a show. This bunch actually lived it.

High school sweethearts, Mark Foleson and Jenny Thompson went to different colleges and pledged to remain faithful to each other. And they were. Because three breakups over the five years that followed didn't count. And when push came to shove, Mark and Jenny knew they were destined for each other.

Twenty-nine years later, people in St. Clair didn't just think Coach Foleson and Jenny were an honest and committed couple, they knew these two *were* completely and utterly devoted to each other. Behind closed doors, the lovebirds were the same people as they appeared to be in public.

Together, they had four children, three of whom were adults and had made names for themselves in school and their chosen careers. Every Sunday, all three made their way home to share a meal and spend the afternoon together. Even on weekends when there were football games to attend and travel involved, the whole family would either go watch their favorite team or spend time with their mom until the others came home.

The oldest was Melanie, twenty-six, who had gone to college for only two years after being invited to join a successful art studio in the city as their artist-in-residence. She designed projects for the municipality as well as private clients. She had continued her studies online before graduating with a master's in occupational therapy, simply because she took after her mother's insatiable desire to study humans. Not to mention the pressure people put on her to have something to fall back on. But her motivation was intrinsic and being multifaceted and well-balanced was something each Foleson seemed to come by naturally.

Timothy was the second, a true middle child, and the town star athlete. He never once played football for his father but instead ran track and field with Olympic dreams. After ending up with a serious knee injury during his last year of high school, Timothy ultimately decided to pursue his true dreams at culinary school. At the age of twenty-three, he was now head chef and co-owner of a new restaurant, Bistro de l'Arte, set to open in the city later that fall.

The third sibling was Brandon who, at six foot six and two hundred and eighty pounds, resembled his father more than any of the children. He was the only Foleson to play on the famed Spartan high school football team. In his third year at the state university only thirty minutes from home on a full-ride athletic scholarship, rumor had it that Brandon was being scouted for the NFL.

Years later came the fourth child no one expected or planned for. Jake. The baby. He was probably viewed as any typical baby of the family in some people's eyes, but not in the Foleson house. He was the glue that kept everyone together. Truly responsible and creative, the other three would joke about how the family "accident" was going to be the most successful, impressive one of the bunch. Jenny couldn't say that she disagreed, but she hated it when they called Jake an accident. "We just weren't *planning* on having another child is all. He's definitely not an accident," she'd insist.

And Jake was Milo's absolute best friend. They had met in third grade when the Connors bought the big house, which meant switching school districts for the kids. Morgan and Jarvis agreed on a few things when it came to parenting, and the public school system was one of them. They couldn't have asked for a better experience when it came to the school, their kids, and the influence the Folesons had on their children.

"You've been thinking about the Connors, have you?" Mark looked at his wife inquisitively.

"Yeah," Jenny paused. "I just... I've been thinking about Morgan and what happened. Jarvis doesn't seem to have any type of remorse. And I just wonder if anyone has even reached out to her, you know?"

"Jen, what do you expect him to do? Express his regret about his marital problems at rehearsal?" Coach winked. "I don't know if you want to get involved," he said.

Coach Foleson already knew where his wife was going with her thoughts. Not one to put his nose in people's business, Coach had a lot of clout in the town and was excellent at maintaining a friendly rapport on every side. He was known as a perfectionist who demanded excellence, but not in a harsh way that would force players into compliance. He was the guy everyone simply wanted to be like. Kind, hardworking, no-nonsense. A man who delivered more wins in his career than any other high school football coach in the state had ever dreamed of seeing. He had been recruited time and again for jobs at colleges and universities all across the nation but remained content where he had chosen to land.

Just after their wedding and for the first eighteen years of his career, he and Jenny had taken care of Coach's ailing mother who had been diagnosed with Parkinson's and dementia. Uprooting her would have been out of the question. At times they had a live-in nurse. When their income wouldn't support it, the two would tag-team, and neighbors pitched when needed. After the state championship wins began to stack up and Coach's salary increased, the two most thoughtful people in the district sought and deeply valued nothing more than a meaningful life in a small town close to the big city. By the time Mama Foleson passed, the family was already revered as hometown icons. Their lives seemed richer and fuller than they could have ever planned.

"I mean, babe, I don't want to tell you what to do, you know that. But you have training in this kind of thing, right? Like giving unsolicited advice or help," Coach continued with a smile.

"Well, I think it's precisely because I *do* have training that I want to attempt to help a little," Jenny explained. "I'm not talking about advice. I'm a high school counselor, not a family therapist."

Mark cut her off. "You are the best therapist this town could ask for and we all know it. You've taken more courses than anyone I know!"

"Well, I can't help it. I love learning about the nuances of the human experience. Did you know-" Jenny was about to explain what she had learned in her latest neuroscience course and what she found problematic about using the term *neuroplasticity,* but instead she hesitated. "Hey, that's not fair. Don't distract me with compliments."

Mark pulled his wife close and kissed her on the mouth. Jenny's knees still went slightly weak when her husband would show his uninhibited affection.

"I can't help myself," he winked again as he released his arms from her waist.

Jenny smiled up at him but was undeterred. "I think we should offer her help. I'm just not sure Morgan and the kids are safe."

Mark backed up slightly, lowering his voice. "Safe? Seriously?"

Jenny nodded without expounding upon the gut feeling she had.

"I mean, fun-loving Jarvis? He doesn't seem to have a care in the world," Mark continued.

"And don't you think that indicates a problem? You saw that Facebook post that he conveniently deleted."

"Only because Jake screenshotted it as evidence," he retorted with a hint of disapproval.

"That doesn't change the facts, honey. He spray-painted the driveway in front of his house to publicly punish his wife! And you can still see bright blue flecks on the pavement."

"That's awful." Mark shook his head. "It does seem rather aggressive."

"It's downright abuse. Can you imagine ever doing something like that to *me?*"

"Of course not," he reacted. The mild-mannered, stoic, gentlemanly side of Coach Foleson was almost offended that his wife would even suggest such a thing. But he knew what his wife was implying. It wasn't in his character. But it was clearly in Jarvis'.

"I suppose we tend to give Jarvis a pass on his little pranks and dark humor. He's always been slightly hyperbolic," Coach said.

"Slightly?" Jenny snorted. "There's a difference between dark humor and cruelty. The former carries a lighthearted message about the difficulties we all face and the latter singles out victims."

"You think Morgan is a victim?" Coach asked sincerely.

"That message wasn't for us, babe. It was a scarlet letter intended for no one but Morgan."

The house was quiet, but Morgan still tiptoed her way through the rooms, gathering only essential items. It had been two days and exactly eighty-three missed calls from Jarvis since she had taken the kids and left. She knew she could be in trouble for it legally. At least, she assumed it was probably true after listening to a few of the voice messages Jarvis left, reminding her that he could have her arrested for leaving with the children without his consent. But it didn't matter at that moment. The kids wanted to stay with her, and she wasn't about to force them to remain in a house where their father was increasingly volatile.

She figured she'd have a total of thirteen minutes—the exact amount of time it would take Jarvis to travel the fastest route home from his closest office—to get in and out of the house. She checked the time on her video doorbell app that started recording when the Uber stopped in front of the house.

She glanced down at her watch. Nine minutes and forty-three seconds. She had plenty of time. One tote bag, a duffle, and a short list of items the kids wanted were nestled in her arms. She grabbed her car keys from the hook by the garage and opened the door. She was taking Milo's soccer shoes from the garage floor mat when her eyes landed on a blue can of spray paint sitting on the shelf. Sucking back tears, she opened the door of her car and tossed the armful of items onto the passenger's seat, letting it fall shut behind her. Slowly pulling out of the garage, she took a long look at the place she had called home for more than a decade. What she assumed would be her cinder block fortress, guarding her from outside perils, became the prison walls of a psychological nightmare. Tears began to flow as she continued backing out, trying to convince herself that she and the kids would be okay.

Holding back a sob, Morgan saw Jenny's number pop up on the screen of her car and decided to answer even if she couldn't fully mask the sound of her crying. It was usually something involving the boys if Jenny called her during school hours, and at this point, Morgan was prone to assume if a person other than Tiffany was calling her, then there was absolutely something wrong.

"Hey, Jenny," Morgan answered, struggling to sound carefree.

"Hi, Morgan. How are you doing?" Jenny's tone was compassionate, giving Morgan the chance to resist overreacting.

"I'm okay. Thanks for asking," she replied. Morgan was not okay. She knew it, and so did Jenny.

"Well, I hope that's true, Morgan." There was a hollow pause in the conversation that neither woman was sure how to fill, but Jenny finally continued.

"I have been thinking about you since you picked Milo up the other night. I mean, I don't want to assume. And I don't mean to pry, but..."

Jenny continued to speak as the words warbled in Morgan's ears. She pulled the car into the parking lot of a gas station along the side of the road. Morgan knew there was no way she could hold it together without concentrating on what she was hearing and saying, and she felt like she was far enough away from the house to come to a stop. Morgan took a deep breath and turned off her car, lifting the phone to her ear and responding to Jenny.

"Is everything okay?" Morgan asked. "Are the boys good?"

"Oh, yes. Nothing's wrong. I was just thinking of asking if you need a job. Like I said, I don't want to assume, but Triston mentioned that there was an incident with you and Judy a couple of weeks ago at church. So, I asked Judy for a few details. I hope you don't mind."

Morgan didn't mind. She would rather have people ask for details than make assumptions. After taking out a few of her frustrations on Judy, a genuinely lovely person, Morgan felt like it was only fair for people to hear about it from the lips of someone who was involved. Triston, the worship pastor who seemed to cut people out of the program without hesitation if any conversation arose that could put them in a bad light, tended to relay gossip as if it was his favorite hobby. Morgan could only be grateful that Jenny went straight to Judy, and then had the decency to call her.

Jenny went on without giving Morgan the chance to reply. "I didn't know you weren't paid for your church job, Morgan. And I'm so sorry they didn't continue to help..." Her voice trailed off.

"Thank you," Morgan said, managing to maintain her composure. In fact, she was feeling stronger by the moment.

"Well, you know Timothy is opening a restaurant in the city, right? I know it'll be a commute for you. But if you need the job, they're looking for a manager."

"But..." Morgan could hardly believe what she was hearing and felt inclined to argue against herself. "I don't have any experience in the restaurant business," she replied.

"I don't think you need it, honestly," Jenny assured her. "You were Jarvis' original office manager when the kids were younger. I remember that and I seriously don't know how you did it all. I can't imagine the restaurant will be more involved than what you've handled in the past," she encouraged.

Though Morgan had a relatively negative view of herself for the past few years, people who knew her for any length of time didn't feel the same way. Perhaps they were guilty of failing to address the red flags. Or of watching Morgan's personality fade without asking if she was all right. Mostly it was because they imagined Morgan to be strong, confident, intelligent, and fierce.

"I... I don't know what to say!" Morgan exclaimed.

"So, do you want the job?" Jenny offered and then backtracked. "I mean, I'm not able to give you the job myself, but I am an investor and consultant for Tim. And you'd be my first recommendation, Morgan. I'm just asking you to apply. That is if you'd like to."

"Thank you, Jenny." Morgan felt warm gratitude fill her heart as a subtle tear trickled down her cheek. No panic, no distress, only release.

Jenny didn't ask for details, for reasons or excuses or explanations about Morgan's side. She was merely offering help. Morgan took in a deep, healing breath.

"I'd love to apply," she confirmed.

"Great. I'll send you an email with the job details and a few dates for an interview this week. Sound good?"

"Yeah, sounds perfect," Morgan replied with overwhelming gratitude.

As the phone went silent, she leaned her head on the back of the seat, letting out a sigh.

"What. Just. Happened?" she said out loud. A smile crept across her face as she allowed a giggle to rise. It had been quite a while since Morgan had celebrated a sincere moment of joy for herself. The mounting temptation to weep had dissipated mid-conversation, and Morgan allowed herself a moment to appreciate the sense of calm she felt.

Her car engine whirred as Morgan pulled out of the gas station, heading down the road with a newfound anticipation. As she approached the acceleration ramp, merging onto the highway, she couldn't help but notice the large billboard with her husband's and Aimee's faces, boasting the best eye care in the area. For the first time in a very long time, Morgan didn't allow the larger-than-life image to intimidate her. She maintained her smile and turned the music up loud. But only a few seconds passed before she saw another call appear on her screen.

"Hey, Johnny," she answered.

Seeing his name illuminated was enough to wipe the smile off Morgan's face. She was healing, growing, and finding moments of hope, but there wasn't an explanation in the world that would allow her to think this call could be positive too.

"Hey, Morgan," he said on the other end. "Can you talk?"

"I'm in the car right now, headed..." She let her voice trail off. She hadn't told anyone where she was staying the past few nights. "I'm doing some running around. Maybe later?"

"Can we meet?" Johnny asked.

"Umm, you sure that's a good idea?"

"Well, what can it hurt now?" he chuckled.

"I guess you have a point." Morgan acknowledged with a smile, her sense of calm returning. *What do I have to lose?* she thought. "Yeah, sure. Let's meet."

Chapter 8
Without Recourse

THE HEAT OF A full-blown Midwest summer had set in without apology. Heavy air carried the weight of lingering rain as tufts of steam lifted from the blistering sidewalks. Morgan didn't mind the heat as she walked along the edge of the street, teetering on the pinnacle of the curb like a daring toddler, taking in her surroundings. There was a slight bounce of anticipation in her step, but she wasn't sure why. She was biding her time. And she knew it.

Rather than driving into the city, she had an Uber drop her off at a café on the corner. Something told her that she shouldn't drive her car if at all possible. Even though she hadn't seen him in weeks and had worked hard to find all the tracking spyware he had on her phone, laptop, and vehicle, Morgan was still a little paranoid that Jarvis would show up without warning. She didn't want anyone to know where she was, much less her soon-to-be ex-husband.

Morgan didn't stay at Tiffany's once she left. A couple of nights were more than enough, given the fact that she foolishly told Jarvis where she was going. Both women felt it was too risky for Morgan and the kids to stay there, and after Jarvis showed up at the apartment door babbling about signing divorce papers and demanding to talk to Morgan, Tiffany was glad she suggested they apply for help at a local women's shelter.

Because another family had just moved out, Morgan, Sadie, and Milo were able to move into a safe house with an undisclosed address less than seventy-two hours after Jarvis' rage-filled explosion. Down a road marked with a *no outlet* sign, nestled between one of the oldest neighborhoods in the county and a budding commercial area, was a three-acre property called *Sarah's House* with a large residence and two outbuildings that could accommodate up to thirty-six people. Local businesses and churches would donate time, money, and goods to help women and children in need, but few knew where the organization was located.

Together, Tiffany and Morgan had volunteered often in that space, from painting and decorating rooms in need of a little upgrade to offering tutoring and music lessons to children. The irony that Morgan would need the services herself was not lost on her. The good thing about being married to a man who threw money at things rather than getting involved was that Jarvis had no clue where the nonprofit was located, even though he had donated thousands of dollars throughout

the years to its cause. And for the two months that had passed
with Morgan and her children behind its walls, she finally felt
a sense of safety.

After a short drive into the city, Morgan was happy to find
herself among streets where she could feel lost among crowds.
People didn't so much as look her way.

"Hey, Morgan!" a friendly voice called out to her.

"Oh, gosh, you startled me," she replied. "I must have been
lost in thought."

"I'd say so. You passed the restaurant a couple of doors
down!" Johnny pointed toward a quaint coffeehouse on the
ground floor of an office tower. "I thought I saw you, so I
figured I should check and stop you before you got too far,"
he laughed.

"Yeah, thanks, sorry. I have an interview just down the
street later today, and I guess I was preoccupied."

As they began walking toward the coffee shop together,
Johnny smiled. "Oh, that's great. Congratulations," he said
sincerely. "It'll be a refreshing change for you in the city, don't
you think?"

"For sure," Morgan responded. She didn't want to elaborate. She didn't need to. They both felt the significance of
meaning behind every word.

As they entered the shop, she noticed a laptop and backpack sitting at a corner table that Johnny was headed toward.

"Oh, have you been here long? I'm not late, am I?" she asked, looking at her watch.

"No, no. I've just been trying to get a little work done. You know, job search and all. It's easier than sitting at my kitchen table trying to get it done," he sighed.

"Yeah." Morgan wasn't able to offer anything more than an understanding nod. "It's taking a while, huh?"

"Yup," Johnny confirmed. "Turns out there's not a lot of demand for a guy who has some leadership experience in the church." He tried to make it sound funny, but Morgan felt the weight of his words in the pit of her stomach.

As they took their seats, the coffeehouse began to bustle with a lively afternoon crowd, people filing in two or three at a time as if everyone needed a pick-me-up snack or drink to complete their work day. Morgan loved the sound of the whirring espresso machine and hoped it could drown out any conversation she and Johnny had, just in case there was a chance a nosy eavesdropper from town would find their way into the space.

After a few awkward shifts in his seat, and Morgan's refusal to be the first one to lead the conversation, Johnny finally spoke.

"So, I thought it would be a good idea to talk."

"For real? I mean, it's good that we're a bit removed from the prying eyes of our beloved townspeople around every corner, but it's not like we're out of the woods," Morgan sighed. "I don't know if it'll ever be a good idea!"

"Morgan, I don't care what people say anymore. Do you?"

"Of course I do. And I think you do too. But it's different for me. I'm not safe. Not anywhere," she stammered.

"I'm so sorry about that. I wish I could assume that you're exaggerating. But I know you're not. Can I help?"

Morgan shrugged. "Yeah, just what I need," she laughed. " Johnny the bodyguard. No one will think anything of that," she teased.

Johnny cast a grin and a wink at her, and Morgan felt her heart flutter. She did care about him and knew he sincerely cared for her. But not everything was sexual. It was, in fact, not about sex at all. It was about a true connection that made her feel safe, unjudged, and unapologetically human. For the very first time, she allowed herself to appreciate what she was feeling for Johnny.

"I was thinking more like helping you move, or if your interview doesn't work out today, I know a few people at the university who can help you if you need a job. I'm kind of banking on them helping me out, but especially if I get in, I think you'd be able to get into the admissions office. And I know you must be hoping to protect your identity, and I think they'd be sensitive to that. I know that's a lot of *ifs*," he paused. "But, I'm on my third interview and I think I'm going to get into the admissions office." He let his eyes wander as if he were searching for his next sentence somewhere in the crowd.

"Thanks." Morgan nodded gratefully. "But is that why you wanted to meet? I mean, you could have said all of this over the phone, Johnny. And if you just wanted to see if I'm angry with you, I'm not. You don't owe me anything."

"Well, that's certainly kind of you." He hesitated before continuing. "But I can't agree. I feel like I do owe you. If not an apology, at least an explanation."

"Okay, that's probably true," Morgan shrugged. She kept her tone light. She didn't have the energy to be upset with Johnny, but she could admit that she didn't understand how their circumstances had led them to where they were.

Johnny had been fired from his job. People were telling her that Johnny had admitted to the two of them having an affair, and she and her kids had been forced to hide out in a women's shelter because her husband also thought they were sleeping together. Morgan chose not to believe the rumors about what Johnny had told people, but deep down, she did let some doubts about him creep in.

"It would be nice to hear your side of things," Morgan admitted.

"I'll start by telling you that I'm sorry that your friendship with me has complicated your life, Morgan," Johnny bega

n. "But you've been someone who has had my back when I needed it, and I wasn't ever going to deny that," he said.

"But why did you tell them we had an affair?" Morgan interjected. "You didn't have to do that."

"I didn't," Johnny explained. "When they asked if I had feelings for you, I answered honestly, that's all."

Morgan felt her stomach flip flop as heat rose to her face. She stirred nervously in her chair.

"I mean, it was just an outburst during their interrogation." Johnny continued, knowing he was making Morgan uncomfortable. He began to rattle off the events at warp speed. "I was called into the office for a meeting with the executive team. They were peppering me with all kinds of questions for what felt like hours. When they asked if we had an affair, I told them the truth. Then they just kept pushing and at one point, when Pastor said, 'But are you too close to Morgan? Do you have feelings for her?' I responded with, 'Of course, I have feelings for her. She's an amazing woman and the only person who has had my back throughout this whole situation.'"

Morgan looked at him stunned. She knew what Johnny was referring to but she hadn't known that church leadership, especially Johnny's former boss, had known as well.

"Oh, Johnny," she said. "Is that why they fired you? It wasn't about me?"

Johnny dropped his head and allowed a tear to escape.

"Oh, it was about everything," he confirmed. "They said that I should have come to them from the beginning instead of confiding in you. But mostly they said they can't trust me with their children if I can't even get a handle on my own."

Morgan pulled her chair closer to Johnny, unapologetically placing her hand on his forearm. "I'm so sorry. How did they find out?"

"She told them. I mean, she literally just told Pastor, 'I'm gay and I think Jesus still loves me, just as I am.'"

"She what?" Morgan gasped.

"Yeah, she's the bravest person I know. When all I've shown her is cowardice." Johnny didn't attempt to stifle his tears as he put his head in his hands and openly wept.

Crying didn't scare Morgan. She leaned in closer and put her hand on Johnny's back. As a volunteer for many years, she was used to consoling people in their times of crisis. In a way, it kept her from the panicky moments of her own anxiety. And she wasn't all that surprised that Johnny's daughter, Hannah, would be so blunt about her opinions.

In the year their family had been at the church, she had grown close to Johnny's sixteen-year-old daughter while Morgan served as her youth leader. In discussions, Hannah would happily share articles and podcasts about translations of the Bible, historical context, and political implications.

She was a striking blend of intellect and compassion, embodying the essence of studiousness and kindness in equal measure. With an insatiable thirst for knowledge, Hannah was often found immersed in books, her curious mind eagerly devouring the intricacies of any subject that piqued her interest. Her dedication to academic pursuits was matched only by her genuine desire to understand the world around her and make a positive difference within it. Despite the challenges she faced as a gay teenager in a conservative environment, Hannah's kindness shone brightly. Her unwavering commitment to both her studies and the well-being of others painted her as a beacon of light in a sometimes dark and tumultuous world.

"Did you know that plenty of Christians are gay?" she stated during one discussion as a group of teenagers, members of the youth Bible study group that gathered on a bi-weekly basis in Morgan's living room, sat wide-eyed one Sunday evening.

Hannah didn't exactly come out to anyone in the church, she was just constantly challenging traditional discussions around sexuality. And her rebuttals were always founded on research.

"Oh, that's interesting that you use the word 'natural' there. We can talk about natural sexual activity if you want. Did you know how many species *do* have same-sex encounters?" she would demand. "Yeah, it's like fifteen hundred or something. You should look it up," she'd say. "National Wildlife Federation. They do good work. It's all documented natural behavior, and I don't think it has anything to do with the human experience of spirituality."

Instead of being the teacher, Morgan was constantly being taught by a girl who found the joy of research by the age of ten. So when, in a whisper, Hannah told Morgan that she knew she was gay from that same age, it didn't surprise her. When parents began to complain that the discussions their teenagers were having in the Connor's home were a bit too progressive for their liking, Morgan went into protective mode. She and Johnny began meeting privately about how to keep his daughter safe in a world where she was increasingly threatened.

"So it's easier for people to start rumors that the youth pastor is having an affair with the woman affirming his gay daughter than it is to examine their beliefs, I guess," Morgan said, removing her hand from Johnny's back and taking his hand into hers. "The official story they're going to tell is they fired you because of an affair?"

Johnny squeezed Morgan's hands and nodded. "Yes."

"Of course it is." Morgan shook her head. "How's Pam?"

"She's okay."

Johnny's wife, Pam, hadn't wanted to move to the Midwest. She was originally from Boston and couldn't imagine giving up life on the coast. But when Johnny told her that he was either going to have to take a massive pay cut or find another job, she agreed to start the nationwide search for a better position. The large church they found in Maryland wasn't exactly home, but it was close enough. Then the pastor's son graduated from college and was miraculously called to be the new youth leader. Suddenly the ten years Pam and Johnny had invested in the church, growing its congregation and reputation as a well-known youth ministry, came to an abrupt end. Their choice was to relocate or be demoted. And though a job title didn't mean much to a guy like Johnny, the pay was a lot less. With rising inflation, two kids, and a mortgage, it made life untenable.

Pam didn't want to believe that job shifting was an intentional attempt by church leadership to push them out, but once she found herself in a drab existence, far from the life she'd known with no friends or family nearby, she couldn't see it any other way. Since their move, most of her time was spent in bed, curtains drawn, battling massive headaches. She let her nursing license expire and had no intention of renewing it to go back to work. In her opinion, the only good thing about living in the Midwest was the cost of living. With the salary Johnny received from the megachurch, their family finally had enough to cover living expenses and even started to put a little money in savings every month, for the first time.

The role of a pastor's wife is often viewed through a complex lens of both job requirements and social expectations within a congregation. While officially she does not have a job description, there's an implicit understanding that she plays a pivotal role in the life of the church. Beyond the expectation to be supportive of her spouse's work, she is seen as a role model for other women in the congregation. There's an anticipation for her to be involved in various church activities, from leading women's groups to organizing community events, all while maintaining a poised and nurturing demeanor. Additionally, she may bear the weight of being a confidante and counselor to congregants, expected to listen with empathy and offer wise counsel. In essence, a church staff wife carries the dual burden of meeting both the practical needs and the emotional expectations of church members. Often without training. All without pay.

But, in a church that size, it's not entirely uncommon for the wife of a leader who doesn't hold the top position to be relatively unknown unless she's on the payroll. For Pam, it was a saving grace. She blended into the crowds, was barely missed by anyone other than the leadership who kept track of staff families' attendance, and leaned into the fact that illness is a forgivable excuse not to show her face.

But when Johnny's boss, Pastor James, pulled him to the side after Pam's three-month absence from church, lecturing him on the expectations of staff wives, she felt obligated to darken the door occasionally. It was only after a little bit of reflection about the logic of her husband having a job requirement that involved her actions being not only bogus but possibly illegal that she let both Johnny and Pastor James know her thoughts on the matter.

"No job description or requirement can ever be met by a third party and therefore would render my attendance concerning Johnny's job completely irrelevant. I'd appreciate it if you leave me out of this," Pam relayed to them both one Sunday morning between the nine o'clock and 10:30 services.

And neither man ever monitored or mentioned church attendance to Pam again.

"And Hannah? How is she?" Morgan asked. "This can't be easier for her."

"No, but I didn't tell her the truth. It's almost more comforting to think that she'll know the story everyone else does. I think it would kill her if she knew what they were demanding. I think it's killing me."

"Gosh, Johnny. What did they expect you to do?"

"They told me I had to choose. They literally said I could choose my daughter or choose my job. My church. That's what they told me."

"*What?* What did they mean by that? Like, kick her out of your house or resign? Tell me they didn't expect you to do that."

"I don't know. It didn't get that far. They just kept asking me if I could still love the sinner and hate the sin. All I could think of was my perfect, amazing daughter, and the long discussions we've had about her not crying herself to sleep at night anymore begging God to change her. Because she knows she's absolutely fine. She realized it all before I did, Morgan."

"I know," Morgan comforted him. "Me too."

"Why do we value ideas over individuals? Why do we justify hate? I can't do it. Not anymore. It's too close to home. It's *in* my home. And I'm sorry I ever believed otherwise." Johnny slumped into his chair, his back finally resting on the cushion. He was empty of any more tears.

"You don't have to, Johnny." Morgan leaned against her chair back and sighed. "You don't have to do any of it anymore. Maybe they did you a favor."

Johnny grinned, not saying a word.

"I don't mean to sound trite," Morgan sympathized, shrugging her shoulders. "Maybe that's not fair. Too soon."

"You can say whatever you want to me, you know that by now. I assume you have the best intention because I know you." He smiled. "You're right, and I know it. But for someone who hasn't had a real-world job since the age of nineteen, it's a little hard to accept currently," Johnny added.

"Well, we're quite the sight, aren't we?" Morgan chuckled. "Two grown-ups, jobless, lacking real-world experience, completely excised from the entire network of people we used to rely on."

Johnny nodded in agreement. "At least you have a job interview, right?"

"Oh, gosh!" Morgan looked at her watch. "I do have an interview," she said, grateful that she still had time before she had to leave. "I've still got an hour, and it's just down the street." She pointed left to indicate which direction she'd be going and let out a long sigh.

"You'll be great," Johnny smiled.

"So will you," Morgan assured.

"Can I still call you? You know, to make sure you're okay? Keep in touch. I don't want to lose another friend," Johnny said.

"Me either," Morgan agreed.

For the remaining time before her interview, Johnny and Morgan sat and chatted as if they had nothing to lose. Because, truthfully, they didn't.

CHAPTER 9
DEPOSIT &
WITHDRAWAL

THE APARTMENT HAD BEEN empty for three days. Tiffany usually had a cleaning crew come through at the end of the school year, but she'd missed the window to schedule a team from the service she typically used. So, she found herself on her hands and knees, scrubbing tile. The bottom floor apartment wasn't as updated as the top living space. She wasn't convinced that her design choices would be appreciated by college students as much as long-term tenants, so she had left the Formica countertops and dated tile. But as she wiped and scrubbed, she had nothing but regret for not replacing the outdated surfaces with slick, modern finishings.

"Aunt Tiff?" A young voice called out, subtly tapping on the front door before entering the apartment.

"Milo? Is that you?" Tiffany popped up from behind the kitchen island that divided the living area from the cooking space.

"Oh, gosh. You scared me," Milo laughed.

Tiffany chuckled too. "What's up, buddy?" Her face flushed with pure pride and joy. She hadn't seen Milo in weeks and was as surprised to see him there as he was to find her decked out in her rubber gloves and apron in the apartment below her own.

"I was just looking for you." Milo paused. "What are you doing?"

"Just cleaning," she said. "It's been crazy trying to schedule cleanings for this place, so I'm stuck with getting it ready to rent out again myself. As if I have time for everything these days!" Tiffany said with a laugh, removing her cleaning gear. She set the items in her hands on the counter and motioned for Milo to follow her.

"Let's go upstairs and grab some lemonade, okay?" she suggested.

Milo took the lead and turned back towards the door he had entered.

"Whaddya got in your hand there?" Tiffany noticed as she finally took a good look at her nephew.

Milo swiveled on his heel and handed Tiffany a newspaper.

"It's what I wanted to talk to you about. Sadie said she told you about the whole DNA thing, right? And I just... I think we have to tell Mom."

Tiffany swallowed hard. She assumed Morgan would've had a serious conversation about the whole thing with the twins by this point, but also understood why she would choose not to. It was tricky, trying to be a good friend and a good auntie at the same time. They walked up the stairs to her apartment as she unrolled the paper and put it on her countertop.

"How did you get this?" Tiffany asked. "Who even buys newspapers?"

Milo chuckled and shrugged, "I dunno. I guess the diner."

Tiffany nodded. "Of course," she remembered. "They do, don't they?"

Just like many other long-lasting customs, the Old Town Diner stocked a newspaper stand with journalism both national and local, just as they had for more than eighty years. They proudly proclaimed their old-standing rituals in every marketing campaign, "The freshest food in town with the oldest traditions around." It was their schtick. The reason people wanted to go to "Old Town," as locals referred to it. If you wanted to feel like the best things in life never change, they got you. And people ate it up. Literally.

"Yeah, I was at the diner with Jake and you know how people just read these and then leave them on the tables?"

"Sure, of course."

"Well, look." Jake pointed to the image of his father standing next to Aimee, his business partner, and his mother, Emily, cutting a ribbon outside of a new building—the eighth of its kind in their optometry chain.

"What is Emily doing here?" Tiffany blurted.

"Right? You tell me."

Tiffany shook her head and picked it up, scanning the article for clues. She quickly returned the paper to the countertop and exhaled.

"I don't know," she pondered. "What does this have to do with the DNA test though? I mean, I know it's odd that she would come here for something the newspaper would cover; she's never done that before. And she didn't even tell her grandkids? But she *is* his mom. You haven't been back to the house, have you?" Tiffany let her stream of thoughts tumble out without trying to make sense of them.

"Well, that's a lot of questions," Milo said. "Which one should I answer first?"

Tiffany laughed. "Sorry. Have you gone back to the house or talked to your dad yet?"

"No, not yet. I mean, Sadie and I were talking about going to the house to grab some clothes. It's been weeks and we can't expect Mom to buy us all new stuff. I mean, just my swim stuff isn't cheap. That is if I keep up with it. I don't know. I'm probably done with swimming-" Milo didn't finish his sentence before Tiffany chimed in.

"Oh, honey, you don't have to give up swimming," she assured him. "We'll figure something out."

"Give up the 5 a.m. practices and the stupid-long meets? I think I'll be okay," he said, trying to act like it wouldn't be a big deal. "Anyway, even if we do go back to the house, he'll see us on the security cameras. Who knows if the codes are still the same? We probably wouldn't be able to get into our own house anyway. How many times did that happen to Mom when she'd piss him off?"

"Oh, Milo." Tiffany couldn't bring herself to say more.

The space to let a fragment of truth sink in was comforting in a way. Somehow an atmosphere can hold the truth about the insidious nature of passive-aggressive behavior and the toll it takes on the humans closest to it. For a child to witness it, and worse, to become accustomed to it, is more than an individual can handle. So the air somehow wraps its shadows around the pain, hurling it far from the intended victim, allowing one to take a breath and move on.

"Well, I've known your dad for a long time. And I think he's more worried about keeping your mom under his control than anything else. Have you tried talking to him? Maybe asking if you can come over and get your stuff. He might listen."

"No. I don't want Mom and Sadie to think I'm betraying them. I dunno... I get all confused when I try to talk to him, you know? He's good at talking you outta stuff."

Tiffany nodded in agreement. Perhaps that was why she and Jarvis never got along. Because she'd always seen right through his act. It would make her feel crazy, at times, like she was the one seeing things that weren't there while everyone else was blind to his obvious arrogance. Classic gaslighting.

"Well, I understand that. But you're his son and I think of all people, he'd be open to letting you in."

"Yeah, well, I don't want to make him think that I'm okay with all of this. Whatever made Mom mad enough to finally leave has got to be about this. And I think Emily's here to help him with everything. Now that we're out of the house and he's issued divorce papers, I think she's here to protect her assets. And if she finds out that we *are* related... Like, he's our *actual* Dad and we can claim some kind of inheritance to her empire? She will *go off.*"

Tiffany flipped the newspaper over, avoiding looking any further at the one face in the world she was actively developing disdain for, and tried a different route.

"Well, I don't exactly know what you mean by 'go off,' but, honey, have you tried talking to your *mom* at all? Why come to me?"

Milo shrugged, showing a hint of defeat he was actively trying to stave off.

"She's always gone," he shrugged. "I mean, I get it. She *has* to have a job. She's been going in for training at that new bistro. But with the drive there and back, plus the late hours... I dunno. I just don't see her much."

Tiffany felt a pang of sorrow sting her heart. She knew it was true. Ever since Morgan had fled, she was in preservation mode for herself and her children. And since the summer was in full swing and classes hadn't been in session for weeks, her children largely had to fend for themselves. The only consolation Tiffany had was that she could fully rely on the twins' strength and support of their mother.

"Well, kiddo, let's just take it at face value for now. Emily is clearly in town for the ribbon cutting at another one of her son's offices. Odd if you know her; not odd in the grand scheme of things."

Tiffany took the newspaper in her hand again, flapping it in the air, waving the image of Jarvis, his co-founder Aimee, and his mother all holding the end of a giant pair of scissors.

"Before we jump to any conclusions about your grandma's intentions or speculate about what's going to happen, let's focus on what *is* happening, okay?"

Milo grinned. "Sure, Aunt Tiff."

"What? I know that smug look. You're just trying to get me to shut up, aren't you?"

"No, I just think it's funny. You and your one-liners. You should make TikToks. 'Let's not speculate on what's *going* to happen'," Milo mimicked in a deep, guttural tone. "'Let's focus on what *is* happening'," he said before returning to his normal voice. "People eat that stuff up!" he smiled, nudging her with a playful push.

"Oh, yeah, just what I need. A Tiktok following," Tiffany chuckled. "But, do you really think Emily is here about the divorce? I mean, your dad is independently wealthy and..." She let her thoughts remain private as her voice drifted again to silence.

"Well, I'm not saying that we didn't live in a nice house, but we also didn't live like the Connors of the South, that's for sure. So, yeah. I think she's here about the divorce. I don't know what they do or what the big deal is down there, but they're pretty protective of it."

"Yeah, what *does* your grandpa do?" Tiffany smirked.

"I dunno," Milo shrugged. "Insurance, or maybe he's a lawyer. It's something to do with both. They told me once and none of it made sense. I didn't ask again."

Tiffany grabbed Milo by the shoulder, pulling him close. After squeezing him, she rubbed his head like she used to do when he was a little kid, and they both had a good laugh.

"You're a complex individual, Milo Connor."

"Okay, *that* doesn't seem like a compliment," he retorted.

"It is. I love that you can understand the deep nuance of things and still be satisfied with not knowing the answers to others," Tiffany said, changing her tone before adding, "You are wise beyond your years, Obi-Wan."

"Ah, my Qui-Gon Jinn," Milo said, deepening his voice and extending both hands. "You flatter me."

Tiffany followed Milo's lead, as they had been accustomed to doing from the time she shared her love of the Star Wars franchise with the twins when they were only toddlers. Her British accent was nothing to be proud of, but she always gave it her best shot.

"Flattery is for fools, Obi-Wan. I speak naught but truth."

Milo broke character, as usual, and snorted a laugh that tempted Tiffany to break. But she had more practice and was therefore undeterred.

"Everytime, Obi-Wan, Every. Time. The master retains her title." She bowed her head playfully and then cracked a smile, abandoning her attempt at an accent. "Let's go get some ice cream."

Morgan pushed the door open slightly before pausing to look over her shoulder. She couldn't help but imagine that someone was following her. It wasn't outside the realm of possibility with Jarvis. He had hired detectives in the past when Morgan volunteered at the kids' school, convinced she was stepping out on him. When she was certain that the coast was clear, she inched her way into the lobby, walking at a pace that would make most people suspicious. Noticing Tiffany sitting in a chair, waiting, allowed her anxiety to subside as she let out a deep sigh and shook her arms.

You've got this, she thought. Morgan was getting better at understanding how to keep herself from showing visible signs of distress in public. Since the day she left, it was as if there was no reason to maintain the mask. No pretense that was worth keeping up. She'd find herself in the aisle of a grocery store, shaking and staring at items on shelves, or at work standing in the freezer trying to remember what she had gone back there to get. Sometimes, she'd be gone long enough for people to notice and they'd send someone to find her. Morgan couldn't quite get a handle on her lack of focus, but at least the trembling had subsided, and she could breathe through stress. And if this day wasn't one of the most stressful of her life, she didn't know what was.

"Hey, you!" Tiffany looked up from her phone, noticing Morgan walking toward her, and stood up to hug her. "You doing okay?"

"Yeah." Morgan nodded. "I'm good. Do we need to check in or something?" she asked, as she released the long-needed embrace from her bestie.

"Oh, yeah, I checked in already. The receptionist said they'd call our name when they're ready for us."

Morgan and Tiffany took a seat in comfy, high-back chairs lining the wall of the lobby in the office building of Norman and Townsley. The firm was known for its tenacious duo, Tina Norman and Shannon Townsley. With a reputation for being the fiercest advocates for women in the state, they indiscriminately represented a diverse clientele. If you were a woman going through a divorce from a powerful man, everyone knew that *this* was where you wanted to be.

Before either of them could say another word, the receptionist announced, "Morgan Connor, please."

Tiffany took Morgan's hand and squeezed. Ever since middle school, the two of them had a code. One squeeze meant *I got you.* Two squeezes meant, *Are you okay?* A rub of the thumb was a *Yes.* And three quick squeezes meant, *No. I'm not okay; let's get outta here.* They even had signs like ear tugging and hair flipping to let the other person know they needed help from across the room. Morgan gently rubbed the side of Tiffany's hand as they followed the receptionist and walked into the office.

A dynamic art deco mural of a woman whose head looked like an explosion of vibrant pink, deep teal green, and or-angey-yellow leaves, flowers, and distorted flourishes embellished the spacious room on one side, with a wall of floor-to-ceiling windows on another. Gold accents caught flecks of each striking color, seeming to bounce off every surface. It was breathtaking. Bold and cheery, yet powerfully strong.

"Morgan?" Shannon Townsley stretched out her hand to grip Morgan's.

"It's a pleasure," Morgan said. "It's nice to meet in person," she continued, as she pointed towards Tiffany. "This is my best friend, Tiffany. I asked her to come with me."

"I kind of insisted, if we're being honest," Tiffany teased as she returned the handshake.

"My kind of bestie," Shannon smiled. "A friend in need, as they say." She nodded with a wide grin.

Shannon Townsley had a way of setting people at ease with a simple glance. She was intimidating, to say the least. Always in high heels, fit and trim with obvious circuit-trained biceps, impeccably dressed for any occasion, Shannon was the epit-ome of a fiery lawyer. But the thing that set her apart from many of her colleagues is that she knew how she came across to people. Her softness was in her smile, in her ability to say things with a grin, letting you know that she cared and cared deeply. She had half-assed nothing in her life. Ever.

The two friends took their seats in the plush yellow chairs situated across from Shannon's desk.

"So, let's chat," Shannon began. "Your husband filed these papers, and we want an amicable separation, correct?"

"Correct. I don't care about any of the stuff. Let him have it all."

Tiffany put a hand on Morgan's knee and jumped in, "Well, let's not be too hasty," she began.

"I agree," Shannon confirmed. "I don't see why we can't watch out for your interests as well as his. We don't have to start a fight, but we need to have our requests nailed down before we have another conversation with his lawyer."

"*Another* conversation?" Morgan was surprised. She didn't think her lawyer had already been in communication with Jarvis' counsel. It made her nervous. Like there was no hiding the fact that she had seen the papers, and this was, in fact, happening. The reality of her situation was enough for her to tear up.

"Mmhmm, I spoke with his lawyer on Friday. I needed to ask him for Mr. Connor's income disclosure, and I requested that he share the proposed division of assets if they have one."

"So, you asked him for that stuff? Already?" It was unsettling, all of it, and no one could blame Morgan for allowing her emotions to surge to the surface.

"Yes. It's standard, Morgan. This will be okay."

"I only want the kids. Let him keep his stupid stuff. The one thing I won't be able to handle is if I get separated from my kids."

"Well, " Shannon began as she rustled some of the papers on her desk. "Yeah, we have an asset proposal from him, I think. His attorney sent it this morning." She continued scanning the documents from the folder her assistant had placed on the desk for their meeting. "Yes, here it is." She took gold-rimmed reading glasses from her desk and placed them on the tip of her nose. "It looks like there's no income disclosure, though. But we do have an idea of what he wants. I'm not going back to his lawyer with anything until we get the truth about what he makes, owns, and has in his bank accounts."

"No," Morgan said. "No need. I just want the kids. He won't fight me on that. Whatever it says on that paper, I'm pretty sure I'm good with it."

"Morgan," Tiffany said in disapproval.

"No, Tiff, you're not gonna talk me out of this one. I'm not fighting him."

"I'm not saying to fight him," Tiffany replied. "I'm saying you need to go back to his lawyer with a strong proposal."

"I agree," Shannon said. "But we haven't even gone over the terms they're proposing, so let's just see what he's offering first, okay? I didn't have time to read these before our meeting, but I figured it was best to go through line by line with you today anyway."

"Okay," Morgan agreed. "Whatever it says, I doubt I'll have much to add."

"That's fine," Shannon calmly assured, "If your main concern is custody, I'm sure there's no reason for him to request anything less than the standard fifty-fifty custody split."

"Fifty-fifty?" Morgan scoffed. "That'd probably be like a punishment for him. He hasn't been what you would call a present and active participant in parenting."

"So, are you saying you want to ask for full custody?" Shannon inquired.

"I'm saying I think he'll assume that I'll take care of them like I always have," Morgan said. "He tolerates his children more than he exhibits any kind of real interest in them," she added with a shrug.

"Well, regardless, giving up full custody also means giving the ex more money for child support. In my experience, men like Jarvis would rather pay people to take care of the kids in his care than pay you directly." Shannon lifted a page, passing it across the desk in Morgan's direction. "And it looks like that's exactly his intention."

Morgan took the paper from Shannon and began fixating on the inky words emblazoned on the stark white sheet. A proposed fifty-fifty custody arrangement, exchanging the children at a mutually agreed upon location once a week, one weekly dinner with Jarvis on the off weeks, and an equal split of holidays between them. Six thousand monthly compensation for all child and spousal support. It was all there, in writing.

Numbness enveloped her like a heavy fog, muffling her senses and leaving her caught in a fog of apathy. She felt hollow and fragile as if the very essence of who she was had been shattered beyond repair. Yet, beneath the facade of stoicism, a flicker of defiance burned within her, a stubborn refusal to let this moment define her.

"Just tell him we accept." Morgan stood, placing the page back on the desk. "I've gotta get to work. And then figure out where I'm going to *live,*" she said as she moved toward the door.

"Mo, c'mon, wait," Tiffany said, reaching for the document. She stared at the information, hardly able to believe it herself.

Morgan paused, waiting for Tiffany to come to the same realization she just had. This was probably her only chance to leave this nightmare of a marriage peacefully.

"Ladies," Shannon asserted, "I see this all the time. He's a man in a really good position and he's likely moving money around as we speak since he didn't include an income disclosure. He's counting on his reputation to be undeterred as he attempts to make this hard on you. Plus, we know he has the funds to get the best lawyers money can buy. Trust me, I'm not cheap either. But I can win for you. It'll cost you—and more importantly, your husband—part of the fortune we're after, but at the end of the day, I am *your* lawyer, Morgan." Shannon steadied her eyes on Morgan, projecting strength and empathy over her entire being. "I will advise you, but I will do exactly what *you* tell me to do."

"Let him have it all," Morgan repeated. "He's already done the worst thing possible by threatening to take my kids away from me half of the time. What can matter more than that?" Morgan remained on her feet during the exchange and began moving quickly towards the door before Tiffany could utter a word.

"Wait. What if his name isn't on the birth certificates? I mean, if there's no proof he's the kids' father," Tiffany blurted.

"Is that true?" Shannon asked.

Morgan's hand froze on the door handle before releasing her grip. She turned to face the two women.

"Yes," she began. "But... You can't tell anyone stuff we discuss in here, right?"

Shannon smiled and assured her, "We have attorney-client privilege no matter where we are."

"Okay, then." Morgan, with a rush of hope, quickly returned to the chair, lowering herself into the deep cushions. "I was pregnant when Jarvis and I got together. He never wanted his name on the kids' birth certificates because his family owns a large fortune down South. His mom wouldn't have been okay with non-Connors making any sort of claim to it. So, he decided that we just wouldn't write his name down as the father. I tried to talk him into not telling his mom I was expecting. But with twins, it's kind of hard to hide. So, he confided in her and she agreed that it was the best way to handle the *situation*." Morgan threw finger quotes into the air, shaking her head. "How messed up is that? And I thought we would have more kids. We tried to get pregnant for years until... Well, I'm the one who gave up. Anyway, he has no proof the twins are his. At least, not really. Sadie and I are the only ones with access to the account..." Morgan let her thoughts drift.

Shannon furrowed her brow, looking confused.

"You gotta tell her the whole thing, Mo," Tiffany pressed.

Morgan nodded in agreement, taking another deep breath before continuing. "Yeah. So Sadie needed her birth certificate for a passport and went digging around for it. Before I could figure something out, she found the original documents in Jarvis' office and saw that no father was listed on her birth certificate, so I had to tell her the truth. But leave it to Sadie." Morgan let a smile flash across her face as she proudly thought about her daughter's strength. "The day I left him, I found out that Sadie took a DNA test. She sent it to one of those online services and found out that Jarvis actually *is* her birth father."

"What?" Shannon gasped. "I don't understand."

"I was raped. We were in college. Before I started officially dating Jarvis, I was raped. And when I found out I was pregnant, he was there for me..."

The lightbulb went off in Shannon's mind. "So you found out that your *husband* is your college rapist only weeks ago?"

Morgan faintly bobbed her head up and down.

Shannon slumped back in her chair, placing her chin in one hand. She had seen a lot in her days of being a lawyer and had heard a lot of stories, especially at dinner parties. She thought she had pretty much heard and seen everything, but this one surprised her.

"Does he know?" Shannon questioned.

"Know what?" asked Tiffany, gently holding her best friend's hand as the tears began to flow.

"Does he know that you *know* he raped you? That he's their biological father?" Shannon clarified.

"Yes," Morgan managed to reply through soft tears. It was strange. Ever since she'd been out of the house, there were fewer bouts of panicked breathing, and instead, a consistent release of pent-up tears. "But there's no way he's going to want anyone else to know. I guess we have leverage," Morgan said, her steely gaze meeting Shannon's.

"I knew I liked you," Shannon smiled. "We can weave subtle language in our proposal to let him know we'll keep his secret, but he has to pay."

"Not money, just the kids," Morgan said with resolve, wiping her eyes, content with the amount of liberation she felt after letting herself cry.

"Okay. We'll start there. He should cover lawyer's fees, though."

"Absolutely!" Tiffany vehemently agreed. "We have other bills to pay, but this can't be her main concern right now. And, the housing thing? Leave it to me, Mo. You guys can live in the apartment. I don't have tenants now, and while you're away, I can be there for the kids. I'll ask the hospital to schedule my shifts around yours, okay? You'll be good."

Turning to Shannon, Tiffany added lightheartedly, "No fight, just a strongly worded proposal, am I right, Ms. Attorney?" she smiled.

"You are, indeed. No fight unless she states otherwise. And, Morgan, I know you may not think it's worth it, but if you ever want to discuss all of your options, when you're ready, I'm here. You've told me from our initial phone call that you aren't interested in anything but an amicable separation agreement. But, here, today, you've mentioned potential crimes we could investigate. If you want to seek justice, I'll always be here."

"Justice?" Morgan squinted her eyes, exhaling a quick huff. "I don't know if I believe in such a thing."

Chapter 10
In Tandem

Sadie rubbed her sweaty palms against her jeans. Even though it was summer, she always felt cold indoors. She wore long pants and carried a cardigan pretty much everywhere she went. So, standing in front of her dad's house—the one she refused to call home after years of using that word—waiting for him to come to the door while a heatwave permeated the air, she was covered in sweat.

She rang the doorbell and waited.

"Sadie, what are you doing here?" Jarvis opened the door and spoke through a bite of food, stifling his annoyance from having to get up in the middle of dinner. Sadie could tell he hadn't checked his phone or watch to see who was at the door. He looked uncharacteristically surprised.

"Hey Dad," she said dryly. "Can I come in?"

"Yeah, sure, of course." Jarvis shuffled himself backward, swinging the door open wide and allowing his daughter to enter.

As she stepped in, she heard Aimee Scott's voice projecting from the kitchen. "Oh, hey, Sadie! How *are* you?" Aimee's cheerful personality made for an awkward moment as she excitedly rushed to greet Sadie. Sadie was entirely unprepared for the hug she found herself in.

"Hey, Aimee," Sadie replied hesitantly. "I just needed to talk to my dad."

"Oh, of course!" Aimee said unreasonably loudly, as she waved her hands in unnecessary gestures. "I'll get outta your hair!" She smiled as she spun herself around and walked back into the other room.

Sadie glanced at her dad wide-eyed.

"Um, we were going over paperwork for the new location," he explained. "We just opened a new office."

"Yeah, I know. I saw it in the news. Too bad my dad couldn't bother to text me or anything."

"What, you would've come?" Jarvis smirked. "To support your good ole Dad?"

Sometimes Sadie wondered why she even bothered to try with him. But, he *was* her dad. Without a single doubt, and yet, one of her closest friends was adopted by a guy who acted more like a father than Jarvis ever had. Though he had always provided for her, there was never a sense of emotional support or connection. Not like what Sadie noticed in other dads and daughters. Jarvis had his assistant send flowers. He gave Sadie little side hugs. He even told people how proud he was of her while in public and showed up for some of the biggest events in her life. He was present, but it never felt like he was actually *there*. She struggled to hold the truth of both things simultaneously, and desperately wanted to believe that the pattern they found themselves in could change.

"Well, it would be nice to at least *hear* from my dad," Sadie retorted.

After returning to the kitchen to get her purse, Aimee exuberantly announced her departure, attempting to offset some of the tension.

"I'll head out now, you two," she said, giving Sadie another unwanted hug, then reaching up to give Jarvis a peck on the cheek. It wasn't uncommon for Aimee to be overly affectionate, but it was the first time Sadie clocked it as strange.

"See you tomorrow," Aimee said with a smile, pausing long enough to notice Sadie's raised eyebrow. "You know, at the office," she clarified.

"Okay see you then," Jarvis said, practically pushing her out the door.

"Was that weird?" Sadie asked her dad when the door was closed. "I mean, why is she having dinner at home with you? And why does she feel the need to say, 'You know, at the office'?" Sadie mimicked in a low-pitched voice.

"Well, you didn't exactly make things comfortable, that's for sure. Everyone is on edge with all of this, Sadie."

"All of what, Dad? The divorce papers you served Mom? People around town are saying she is divorcing you, the *poor Doctor Connor*. What about all the time she spent in the guest bedroom? Who asks about that? Or the nights she'd come to your door crying, begging you to talk to her? Asking to work things out, begging you to tell her how she could *possibly* please you?"

Jarvis's expression shifted from annoyed to defensive. He crossed his arms, directing an icy stare at his only daughter.

"What has she told you?" he insisted.

"What? Mom hasn't had to say a word. You didn't think we could hear you?" Sadie prodded. "Our walls aren't thick enough to hide what has been going on with you guys for years. We're almost sixteen years old, Dad. You think I didn't notice on my own?"

"What I think is that we should have a civilized conversation," Jarvis said, firmly articulating each syllable. "Can we at least sit on the couch?" he motioned.

"I guess," Sadie replied, determined to keep her stance. Like any skilled fifteen-year-old, she was a pro at maintaining her state of dispassion in the heat of conflict. She would only break her icy facade after hiding away for a time, seeking solace in moody music or YouTube videos. But not many could outlast her dad. He was known to break the most rigid competitor.

They sat opposite from one another, each wondering if the other would speak first, until they heard banging on the door.

When Jarvis first had cameras installed at the house, Milo downloaded the app connected to the security system and then promptly forgot about it. He remembered it once things started to go sideways. He didn't love getting constant notifications, but when he began to feel more and more protective of his mom, he made sure to have access. So, when his twin sister rang the bell, he had a live video feed of her standing on the porch and had listened in as much as he could before the front door closed behind her. Sadie hadn't told him she was going to confront her dad without him, but the second he viewed her image on his phone screen, he made a beeline to his bike and headed there himself.

"Milo, what's up?" Jarvis said with a smile. "You and your sister on the same day?"

Milo suddenly became conscious of the fact that his dad would likely block him from the security app if he let on that he could still sign in, so he thought on his feet.

"Yeah, we share our locations and since she wasn't answering her texts, I thought I'd stop by," Milo said with a toothy grin.

Sadie rolled her eyes. "Smooth," she mouthed behind Jarvis' back.

"I'll get us some lemonade," Jarvis exclaimed. He was clearly delighted to see his son. "I made your favorite! Fresh-squeezed lemon with mint sprigs and honey."

Jarvis was much more fatherly with Milo than he ever had been with Sadie, so it didn't exactly surprise her that the moment her brother walked in, they were treated with hospitality. As Milo approached the couches in the spacious great room, and Jarvis headed into the kitchen, Sadie gave her brother a disapproving look.

"What?" he whispered. "Why are you looking at me that way? What are *you* doing here?" Milo insisted.

"I just wanted to talk. I thought..." Sadie didn't finish her sentence because she didn't quite know *what* she thought.

Did she believe there was a chance her dad would be sorry for what he'd done? Take back everything he'd ever said or done to them? Did she even want that? Did Milo? Did her *mom?* Were they ever really a happy family? She suddenly didn't know what she was doing there at all.

"Well, it can't hurt to talk," Milo comforted his sister, placing a hand on her knee as he watched the wheels of her mind spin.

Jarvis returned with a small tray and three crystal glasses with fresh lemonade adorned by a mint leaf and a perfect lemon wedge. Appearance was always something he paid attention to, and Sadie recognized exactly where she got her eye for detail. She couldn't help but feel a twinge of disdain for the inherited quality and her propensity to be paralyzed by perfectionism at times. She was astute enough to see that the traits went hand in hand, and instead of appreciating her talent, allowed herself to momentarily hate her predecessor. It surprised her what emotions a lemon slice could evoke.

"Thanks," Sadie said quietly, reaching for the glass and lifting it to her lips. She breathed, feeling her resolve waning.

"So, " Jarvis began. "Sadie, you were saying?" He flippantly passed the ball back into her court, sipping on his lemonade and crossing one leg over the other.

"Erm, well," Sadie hesitated before tapping into her courage again. She leaned forward, looking her father squarely in the face. "I just wanted to say that this sucks. You have put us in a terrible position, and we're your kids. Your biological children." She was the one emphasizing syllables now.

Jarvis sat nonplussed, apathetic, and ready for confrontation. "So, that's what this is about? You're my biological children. And you want money."

Though many would frame the words as a question, Jarvis did not. He stated it as if it was a fact.

Sadie scoffed, "Are you serious right now? I thought there just might be a chance to appeal to your soft side! Like, you know, maybe *not* throw us out like you don't even care after all these years. But I mean, maybe it's to be expected since this was all a lie!"

"You *left!*" Jarvis raised his voice. "You went with Mom, and you want to try to blame me?" he demanded.

"You were in a rage!" Sadie shot back.

Milo looked at her, confused. There were a few things she hadn't confided in her brother. She felt some kind of obligation to his more desirable relationship with their father. She didn't want to be the reason Milo looked at their dad in another light. So, she hadn't divulged any particulars about what she had witnessed the night they picked him up from Jake's house, other than Mom had finally had enough and they needed to leave because Dad was mad.

Jarvis didn't care to deny Sadie's claims. He didn't need to. No one would believe a teenager over an adult man who appeared to be the picture of decorum at every turn. But, Milo didn't doubt his sister. He had seen his dad lose control on the golf course when they played together in the father-son league. It wasn't all the time, but when it happened, everyone took notice. Sure, some of the other dads would toss their clubs in the air or kick the sand in the bunkers when they got stuck in a sand trap. Jarvis would hurl his club into the trees, screaming the f-word so loudly people on the next green would turn to see the commotion. And no one would say a word. He was a respected doctor who was simply a fierce competitor as well. Who would think that his rage was anything but an expression of his ambition?

Jarvis leaned forward, determined not to let his daughter rattle him. He lowered his voice.

"Look, I plan on taking care of you in every way, kids. But you're the ones who left with your mother. Let's let the lawyers chat about the specifics. If you want to come home instead of staying God-knows-where, then come home. But don't act like you can understand what happens between a man and his wife. We're getting a divorce because life happens."

The twins sat absorbing their father's words. It's funny what a person does when faced with information. They say there are two sides to every story, but especially in a divorce, the truth is that there are as many sides as there are people affected by it. Milo was tempted to swing from unadulterated hatred to apathy.

"Why did you do it?" he finally spoke.

"Do what?" Jarvis asked, surprised at the reaction.

"Hurt Mom? I mean, you raped her! Why did you even marry Mom? Was it because you knew the baby was yours? *We* were yours? And the only way you could control a situation is if you kept her close? And why hide it for all those years? Acting like you were some kind of savior to her, but never telling the truth? Was it to protect the money? Did you *ever* love her?" Milo asked as he unintentionally allowed the heaviest emotions he'd ever felt to come gushing to the surface.

The halls of an average high school furnish chaos like few other places on Earth, and St. Clair High was no exception. Sadie clenched her backpack tightly. She didn't have a class right then and knew she could skip her study hall without anyone noticing. Study halls were often assigned as volunteer hours to students who served as teachers' aids or helped in the office. Even though she didn't have a hall pass to explain her absence, she knew her teachers would give her the benefit of the doubt and assume she was exactly where she needed to be.

It wasn't the greatest system in the world. Teachers had to place a bit of trust in the students since they were excessively outnumbered. The entire county had one solitary high school that enrolled all kids within a radius of nearly eighty square miles. Since St. Clair was the largest of the small cities in the area—with things like stop lights, restaurants, and parks—kids from the whole region were bussed in for schooling, which made the student population large. Teachers who were willing to spend their careers there were somewhat difficult to come by, but those who stayed were fiercely committed, with a passion for small-town life and an unparalleled devotion to education. And when people would come from all over the state, including the big cities, to see the St. Clair Spartans play football—well, the electricity that permeated their small town would reinforce any educator's decision as well worth it.

"Hey, there, Ms. Connor. What's goin' on?" Coach Foleson tapped on the locker next to Sadie.

The bell had rung, the chaos now at a lull as students remained behind their classroom doors. Instead of walking outside, Sadie stood with her back to a locker, holding onto her bookbag for dear life.

"I..." Words seemed impossible.

"Hey, let's get you to my wife's office, how about that? Do you need help?" Coach asked. "You can take my arm," he offered.

Sadie shook her head, steadying her breath. She didn't want to take Coach's arm. She didn't want to need the help, but as she pushed herself off of the cold metal, an unsteadiness overtook her, and before letting herself tip sideways, she grabbed his arm.

"It'll be okay," Coach said, catching her with his other hand. "We'll go slowly."

Sadie began to sniff small puffs of breath through her nose. It seemed like the only thing she could manage to do at the moment. Walking was challenging. Breathing was challenging. Her vision was blurred and it seemed unlikely that she'd make it another step when Coach put his hand on her elbow, helping lower her to the chair outside an office marked *Jenny Foleson*. He tapped on the door, not waiting for an answer before poking his head in.

Though Coach had spoken to the office staff as they were walking into the counselor's wing, explaining that he needed to see his wife ASAP, Sadie hadn't heard a word of it. Her whole world was a swirling, mumbling, undecipherable mess.

"Hey, babe. Marlene said that you guys are dealing with a crisis, but I need your help *now*." Coach lowered his voice to a whisper, "Cuz we're about to have another one on our hands if we're not careful."

Jenny's eyes widened, motioning for him to come inside, without saying a word. He hadn't noticed that his wife had been holding her desk phone to her ear until he heard her say, "Yep. They are on their way," before placing the receiver down again.

"What's the emergency?" she asked. It was an impressive skill Jenny had, being able to manage two different conversations at once.

"Sadie Connor is in the hallway. I don't think she's okay."

"Sadie? What? That can't be right." Jenny's shock was unmistakable. "You can't be joking, though," she said aloud as if to convince herself.

"Of course, I'm not joking," Coach replied. "I think she's having a panic attack and needs your help, like, right now."

"Mark, Milo Connor is in Mr. Miller's office next door," she sighed deeply. "They found him in the locker room during gym class. They think he was trying to make himself a noose. The ambulance is on its way."

"Oh my God," he gasped. It wasn't often that Coach Foleson would show emotion, but he swallowed hard, choking back a tear. "You take Sadie, okay? Are you going to ride in the ambulance?" he asked.

"Yeah, of course," Jenny answered.

"Well, talk to Sadie now before they get here, okay? You probably don't have long." Coach kissed his wife on the cheek, "It'll be okay. These kids are in good hands."

Days like this were difficult, but it was what kept Jenny passionate about her vocation. She was making a difference, and there was daily evidence. It was hard and heavy sometimes, but she was instrumental in saving young people's lives, literally and figuratively, and it drove her to be committed to being the best version of herself every day. She wasn't flawless, though most people imagined her to be.

"Hey, Sadie." Jenny crouched in front of her before asking, "Is it okay if I put my hands on your knees? Sometimes it can help regulate."

Sitting calmly in front of Jenny's office comforted Sadie enough for her not to feel like she was going to hyperventilate. She nodded, consenting to the offer as Jenny gently settled her hands on top of Sadie's knees.

"Do you want to come into my office?"

Sadie was able to spit out a whisper. "Yes," she said before standing upright and steadily walking into the space.

"Mrs. Foleson, " Sadie began once the door was closed, "I just...I was about to walk out. I wanted to leave school, and then it's almost like things went black." Sadie surprised herself when she was able to speak in full sentences. "Thank God Coach was there."

"Yeah, I'm glad of that too," Jenny said as they both took a seat in chairs next to one another. "But, honey, I need to know what's goin' on. Because I have something to tell you, and it's not good. I wanna help you stay calm, but if I don't know what you're dealing with right now, I feel like I'll be leading you blind, you know?"

"I dunno," Sadie said honestly. "I just... Everything's messed up. We moved into Aunt Tiff's place. Milo and I tried to talk with our dad. Everyone in this town thinks they know everything. And I don't know. It's all fake. Everything. I don't know what to do," Sadie said through a stream of tears. She felt heat begin to rise from her stomach to her head as her breath narrowed.

"It's okay. I understand. Take as deep of a breath as you can, okay? Slow and steady," Jenny instructed. "Well, I'm glad you told me. Thank you. But now I need your help with something, all right?" Jenny kept a hand on Sadie's arm.

"Okay, yeah," Sadie nodded. The thought of being needed focused Sadie's attention. "Is there something else wrong?"

"Yeah, sweetie. Let's just take another breath," Jenny took Sadie's hand. She didn't want to continue withholding such important information from Sadie about her twin, but first, she had to make sure Sadie could keep her cool. "It's Milo. We had to call an ambulance. Are you feeling strong enough to ride with me to take him to the hospital?"

Sadie's determination to get past her swirling thoughts at the moment suddenly fortified with the awareness that her brother was in need.

"*What?* Why? Has he been injured?" Sadie cried.

"No, he's okay. We'll let you see him now, all right? He can tell you the whole story."

"Yeah, yeah, I'd like to see him," she agreed. "Can we go?"

"Of course," Jenny smiled. She could sense the caretaker in Sadie overriding any anxiety as she led her to the office where Milo was sitting. "Hey, Mr. Miller," Jenny began, but the siblings didn't hear another word. Milo fell into his sister's arms, sobbing.

"It's okay," Sadie comforted. "It's okay, I got you," she repeated again and again.

Sadie took Milo's hand. "I think you'll like it," she assured her brother. "You're ready, I promise. You're *really* good."

Milo smiled hesitantly at Sadie. It wasn't like him to lack confidence, but after having the most public breakdown a high schooler could imagine, it was his first week back in school. For two full weeks, they held him at a facility where Sadie and Morgan could visit and attend counseling together. They even allowed them to stay overnight in a private room. It was known to be the best mental health facility in the area, partnering with participating family members and caregivers as part of their protocol. And even though when the ambulance dropped him off Milo wasn't able to fully answer key questions about what had happened, by the fourth day he was crystal clear about his regret and communicated his readiness to participate in any program that would get him home fast.

But going back to school was challenging, to say the least. Now, standing in the hallway with his sister outside the choir room, waiting to go into an audition seemed a bit absurd. Aside from when Sadie was in school, he hadn't been without his twin by his side since she rode with him to the hospital in the back of a whirring ambulance. He wasn't ready to spend more than fifty-two minutes of a class period without her if he didn't have to, so her school theater extracurricular activities were about to become his. If they'd have him. Besides, when Sadie told him that the best revenge was going to be standing on stage for all to see, belting out songs that would make the audience cry while everyone expected him to hide his face, he couldn't deny that it sounded like a pretty epic move.

"Thanks," Milo said. "I mean, thanks for everything. I couldn't ask for a better sister."

"I know," Sadie winked. "Now get in there and blow them away."

And so he did. The guy whom everyone assumed was nothing but a pure athlete walked into the choir room and performed a monologue from *Twelve Angry Jurors* and a song from *Singing In The Rain* to four teachers and three student officers, without missing a beat.

"How'd you do?" Sadie asked when Milo poked his head out of the door again, and then pushed himself past the line of fellow auditioners. "I mean, I heard a little, and your voice sounded great," she said excitedly.

"What did you do, put your ear to the door?" Milo laughed.

"Yeah, of course I did!" Sadie admitted.

"I think I did okay. Man, that felt good."

"I told you!" Sadie smiled, nudging him on the shoulder. "You're a natural. They'll cast you for sure. I mean, even if you don't get a main role, the ensemble is super fun. But you'll get it. I know you will."

Milo wasn't feeling quite as confident about his performance as his sister, but he was hopeful. And it felt pretty amazing to know that after believing that he was completely devoid of hope, there was a shift in his mindset that he couldn't quite explain. It was as if the second he was found in the locker room, a light switch flipped, offering him what he needed to see past the darkness he felt immersed in. A sticky mire had wrapped itself around him, convincing him of a pointless existence. It wasn't exactly washable, but now he saw a path illuminated for him, just in time. He knew there was a way out of the chasm he'd been drowning in.

"Thanks, sis. I love you," Milo kissed her cheek.

It was enough to make her tear up. Sadie had pushed her own anxiety into the background over the past month, but something in her had changed too. The counseling sessions she got to share with her mom and brother, plus the therapy she received individually, all part of the doctor's prescribed familial care plan, was not something she expected, but she was extremely grateful for it. Every family member had made major strides in the few weeks they had treatment. Except Jarvis. His insurance didn't deny the claim, approving care at the facility for the entire family, but he never once showed up.

"I got you, little brother," Sadie chuckled, wiping a tear from her eye. "I got you."

CHAPTER 11
SOLO

A CRISP FALL BREEZE prickled the air as an orangey sun billowed through the large open windows of the Connor home. Milo and Sadie had started off the school year a little rocky, but finding their new place in the strange hierarchy of high school wasn't entirely out of reach for them. Though some of their classmates and neighbors still gossiped in secret, for the most part, people kept quiet about the previous scandal. It seemed the Connor family's lives had begun to settle.

"Don't take that," Jarvis said, looking up momentarily from his laptop and pointing to the lamp Tiffany had her hand on. "Everything you can take has a post-it on it, and I'm pretty sure there's nothing in this room."

"Got it," Tiffany said sharply, lifting a hand to her forehead in a feigned salute. She shifted her weight to her heels and pivoted to walk back into the great room, rolling her eyes. It wasn't even worth whispering her frustrations about Jarvis under her breath. *He* wasn't worth it.

During the few weeks that had turned summer into autumn, Morgan found her stride at the bistro, the kids celebrated their sixteenth birthday—the first without their father present—and Tiffany worked on finishing a few of the updates she had always planned to improve at her rental. Though the shelter had been a lifesaver, Morgan could now afford a small apartment, knowing it would stretch her tiny budget. And Tiffany wasn't kidding about her offer to house her favorite trio. The two friends negotiated a price, but their system of bargaining was anything but traditional. Tiffany kept insisting that rent be lower, while Morgan demanded an agreement that if she ever secured a better job, Tiffany would increase the price. Once they agreed, the only thing left to do was talk to Jarvis about getting furniture and some of the possessions necessary to start a new life from the place that housed her old one.

But, Morgan's divorce had stagnated. She rarely heard from her lawyer and tried not to call or email the office because every time she saw the balance of charges, it would make her heart drop. She was putting her faith in Shannon Townsley, hoping to have the battle go her way, but she couldn't be sure. Add attorney fees to housing and normal living expenses, and it was enough to make a woman doubt herself. But, she didn't have a choice. Morgan knew she wouldn't be able to afford all-new furniture on her own, so she petitioned to collect goods from their formerly shared living space and waited to be granted entry to the premises.

When the day came that Morgan, the kids, Tiffany, and a couple of ER nurses from Tiffany's work rallied to help, bringing a mid-sized moving truck and a few empty boxes to fill up, Jarvis sat in the broad sitting nook that opened to the great room, tapping on computer keys and gazing onto the front lawn from his favorite chair. The lengthy window was tipped slightly open with sheer ivory drapes, rippling from the gentle breeze, offering Jarvis a perfect view of the U-Haul parked in the street. Pulling up and onto the driveway hadn't been cleared, so Morgan didn't even risk it. Piece by piece, the group gathered a few of their possessions from the house, carrying them to the road, and loading belongings into the truck while strategically placing each item in a way that would leave room enough for the next.

At least Jarvis had set out the moving dolly for their convenience. Part of Tiffany wanted to believe that Jarvis could be reasoned with. And then things like this would happen. He sat silently, while people buzzed around him, ignoring their presence unless forced to acknowledge that someone would dare do anything he'd disapprove of. Even when Jennifer, one of Tiffany's colleagues, asked if she could grab water from the fridge, Jarvis remained silent, not even lifting his head to look at her. Tiffany had to walk to the cabinet where the cups were, fill it with ice and water, and help her friend get a drink after hours of labor. By the time the sun sat low, threatening to shorten daylight with the passing of every minute, Tiffany was nearly at her wit's end.

"Dude, we've been here since noon, and I don't think he's gotten out of that chair once," Tiffany said, stomping into the master bedroom closet.

"Shhh," Morgan admonished. "He'll hear you."

"I don't care if he does at this point," Tiffany replied.

"Gosh, what's gotten into you? What is this, role reversal? I'm supposed to be the raging lunatic, right?"

Tiffany chuckled. "You know, that's pretty reductionistic," she gibed.

Morgan shrugged, and without saying a word, handed Tiffany a hanger, pointing to a box by the closet door.

Shaking her head, Tiffany took the hanger, tossing it into a box with the others.

"This sucks, Mo," she said, lowering herself to the closet floor, and removing another one of the hangers from clothing items Morgan had stacked in neatly organized piles. "He can't be bothered to stand up and help you? There's a Post-it on all your stuff. I mean..."

Tiffany's voice trailed off. She stood up again, scanning her surroundings in near disbelief. It had been more than a decade since she had found herself in her best friend's closet, and she took a second to allow herself to take at the moment.

"What in the world are you gonna do with all this stuff?" she asked, lifting a floor-length gown from the rack as the red sequins glinted in the light. Even Morgan's closet had two narrow windows from ceiling to floor and one overhead skylight offering the perfect setting for anyone trying on clothes in the space.

Morgan shook her head and stepped closer, unloading the heavy garment from Tiffany's hand, and returning it to the hanging rack.

"Nothing. I am not going to do anything with it, Tiff. This is what I'm taking," she motioned, circling her hands above the stacks of clothes and shoes. "I don't need anything else."

Tiffany sighed. "Yeah, there's no Post-it anyway," she mocked. It was nice to find a little humor in the absurdity of the situation. "Jarvis will need it for his next event anyway."

The friends chuckled for a moment until their smiles rolled into giggles as if they were thirteen again, joking about a boy who had teased one of them.

"What's so funny?" Milo asked, popping his head into the closet.

"Oh, nothing. Your mom and I were just looking for some Post-it-note approval on these ballgowns." Tiffany laughed. "Guess your dad needs them more than she does."

And Morgan laughed again too, letting out a snort that was threatening to whirl into an uncontrollable guffaw.

"Oh my," Milo said in a grown-up voice. "Do I need to split the two of you up?" he asked, as if not joking at all.

"Nah, we'll be good," Morgan answered, swallowing back another cackle, and approached her son to give him a little peck on the cheek. "Promise," she smiled. "What's up?"

"Well, I have my bed and Sadie's but I wasn't sure if we're taking one for you and I didn't want to ask Dad," Milo said, sounding a lot less grown-up.

"No, it's fine, you don't have to. I emailed him about taking the guest bed, and he didn't exactly reply, so I'm assuming it's fine."

"Well, if there's not a Post-it, I'm not even asking. I'm just gonna load it," Milo said plainly.

"Okay, that's fine. But you'll need help. It's a king-size bed. It breaks down pretty well, but the mattress will have to go on top of some of the other stuff that we have towards the back of the truck," Morgan explained. "Let me finish these two boxes and we'll come and help you, okay? What's Sadie doing?"

"She, Jennifer, and the other lady..." Milo paused, "Sorry, what's her name again?"

"Amber," Tiffany answered.

"Yeah, that's right, Amber. They're all in Sadie's room. I think she's taking everything, Mom," Milo said impatiently, tattling on his sister. He was less attached to his stuff than Sadie was and didn't quite have the tolerance for her sentiment at the moment. His mission was to get in and get out that day, and they had already spent twice the amount of time he hoped they would at the house.

"Let her process, Milo. She's fine. You just help with the bed," Morgan grinned.

"All right. I'll get the tools and start breaking it down," Milo said before leaving the room.

"Thank you, son!" Morgan called out loudly enough for him to hear as he exited the bedroom altogether.

Casting a look of knowing at one another, the two women chuckled again after he was gone and busily returned to their task. Tiffany began to arrange shoe boxes next to a larger one filled with sweaters and scarves when she noticed a rattling sound in one of them.

"Oh, do you want me to take shoes out of these smaller boxes to pack them up all into one big one?" she asked as she lifted the lid on the shoebox in her hand.

"No, let's keep them," Morgan began before pausing, as she looked over at Tiffany's face. "What?" she asked.

Tucked into the corner of the shoebox in her hand was the smallest gun Tiffany had ever seen, bumped up against chunky black wedges.

"Mo, since when do you have a gun?" she gasped.

"Well, technically it's a pocket pistol," she shrugged.

"Okay, since when do you have a *pocket pistol?*" Tiffany grimaced, emphasizing each word.

The two women had been devoted pacifists since they were girls, even committing to vegetarianism for a full year together, until they spent time on the volleyball team and couldn't resist indulging in a victory burger with the players after a win one evening. Even after they decided that they could be okay with their participation in the food chain, Tiffany couldn't imagine Morgan shooting a gun even once in her life.

"Jarvis got it for me when he was doing all that traveling for the classes he'd taught years ago. Now, he doesn't have to go to them, they come to him," Morgan said, reminding them both that the man sitting in the other room had more influence than they could measure, letting the weight of the fact settle in on them like a heavy cloak. "It's been tucked away in this shoebox for the past five years, probably. I took classes and everything. I'm a pretty good shot," Morgan declared, adding to Tiffany's astonishment.

"Well, I'm probably the last person you'd expect to hear this from, but perhaps it's time to return the pistol to its rightful position," Tiffany stated, finally removing it from its place and handing it to Morgan. "You have a pocket, right?" she shrugged.

"Tiff, it's not even loaded," Morgan explained.

"All the better. No one but you and I will know that fact. And it'll make us both feel safer, I think."

Morgan sighed, looking dejectedly toward Tiffany, ultimately taking the hand-sized weapon from her and placing it in the small pocket of her jeans.

Morgan threw her shoes into a small basket next to the floor mat, tiptoeing her way to the bedroom, trying not to wake the twins. She had been working every night as a manager at the restaurant for the nearly two full months it had been in operation, slipping into the apartment in the early hours of the morning, well after the kids had gone to bed. Things were about to change, though. She would be working three daytime hours Monday through Thursday, then weekends during the busiest nights of the week. It still wouldn't give her a day off, but she was happy to put the time in for the little start-up.

Business had kicked off with a bang, making Bistro de l'Arte one of the most sought-after new spots in the city. Word of mouth had spread like wildfire and it helped when they appeared on popular local morning shows, highlighting the area's exclusive new spot for French cuisine. Morgan was tired but happier than she'd been in a very long time. Milo and Sadie spent every bit of time they could with her, even coming to the restaurant just to sit and do homework on the days they didn't have theater rehearsals. Jarvis' lawyers had readily agreed to the requests Shannon had made on Morgan's behalf, and the kids remained with Morgan full-time except for every other weekend. The child support was enough for them to live comfortably since Tiffany didn't charge her any more than she would charge a couple of college students, and though the three-bedroom apartment was a much tighter fit than any of them were used to, it became their happy place.

"Momma?" Sadie whispered before Morgan made it to her bed.

Morgan jumped. "Oh, gosh, honey, you scared me," she whispered, clapping her hand to her heart. "I'm getting too old for people to sneak up on me," she laughed. "What's up, baby? Is everything okay?"

"Yeah, I just had a bad dream. Can I sleep in your bed tonight?" Sadie asked.

"Of course, sweetie," Morgan assured her, as the mother-daughter pair climbed into the sides of the bed, pulling the comforter to their shoulders, hoping the fall chill in the air would help them dream away the rest of the night without interruption.

The two quickly drifted to sleep, securely resting in the haven of each other's presence. The night passed more quickly than desired, and before the morning sun could peek through the windows, a loud banging startled them all awake.

"Shhh, baby. You stay in bed," Morgan told Sadie quietly. "I'll get it."

"Mom, no. Don't go out there alone!" Sadie protested. "It can't be safe!"

"Sweetie, it just sounds like your dad. I'd know that knock from anywhere. You go back to sleep," Morgan said.

"Mom," Sadie let out a pleading sigh, knowing it was useless to try to convince her mom to rethink going to the door.

The loud thumping continued as Morgan pulled a house robe around her body, tying it snuggly at her waist.

"I'm coming!" she called out at a reasonable volume before opening the doors.

Morgan was hoping that she'd be able to keep from waking Milo by staying as quiet as possible. He was the soundest sleeper of the family with hilarious stories of making people think he was awake by fully conversing with them while still

in a moderate slumber, then having no recollection that anyone tried to wake him, or what he had said to convince them
to leave him alone.

She hoped, rather than believed, that he wouldn't be awak-
ened by the commotion. Because living in a state of unknown, nothing seemed stable. Not to her or the kids. Morgan couldn't count on anyone's behavior being defined as
typical.

She peered through the peephole and saw her soon-to-be
ex with fist raised, banging rapidly on the door. Turning the
knob, she took in a deep breath and sighed.

"What are you doing here?" she said before Jarvis could
speak.

"What is this?" Jarvis demanded through gritted teeth as he
waved a paper in the air. He pushed himself past her and into
the apartment.

"Jarvis, it is 5:45 a.m. and I got in from work at one o'clock
this morning. *What* are you doing here?"

"What am I doing here?" Jarvis kept his voice low, his heart
pounding against his chest like a drum in a thunderstorm. He
knew Tiffany could likely be in the apartment above them,
but was holding out hope that she was on a shift at the hospital and wouldn't interrupt his plan to confront Morgan and
the kids. He forced himself to keep from screaming wildly.
It wasn't exactly his style to show outrage in conventional

displays of furor, but such tactics had begun to entice him. He had never battled with his temper so much in his life. Morgan tested every nerve, leaving Jarvis teetering on the edge of desperation.

"What in the world were you thinking?" he spat through his teeth as he slammed the papers onto the kitchen island.

"Dad? What's going on?" Milo asked, sleepily emerging from his room. Sadie peeked her head from the door of Morgan's bedroom, spotted her brother, then rushed to join him.

"C'mon," she whispered. "Let's just go and let them talk for a second."

"Go back to your room, Milo," Jarvis demanded. He hadn't even noticed Sadie emerge to retrieve her brother and paused for a moment as his children slunk back behind a closed door.

For the first time, Jarvis took a look around. He had never been in Tiffany's apartment, much less the rental beneath her own living space, and finally realized the need to take in his surroundings. His face contorted in disgust.

"So, this is what you've been reduced to?" he scoffed. "Did you even provide a bedroom for your kids?" He stared daggers at Morgan.

"Jarvis, if you came here to insult me, I'm going to insist that you leave," Morgan replied.

It was as if she was listening to herself disembodied, telling Jarvis the things she had wanted to say for years, yet hadn't managed to do before.

"Insult you?" Jarvis mocked. "I don't have to waste my time trying to insult you, Morgan," he said. "I am here to accuse you."

"Of what?" Morgan asked in disbelief. "You can't possibly have more accusations." Morgan's nervous laughter oddly felt appropriate in the moment. "You really are something else."

Jarvis nudged the paper on the counter closer to Morgan, who had situated herself smartly between him and the other side of the counter. She picked it up, beginning to read, knowing it wouldn't be long before Jarvis could no longer subdue his rage.

"What were you thinking? You're trying to blackmail me? *Me?*" He finally raised his voice.

"Jarvis, I don't know what you're talking about, but if this is about the divorce, you're the one who said that we should let the lawyers handle it," Morgan reminded him.

"Yeah, great. Let the lawyers handle our custody and estate agreements. Fine. But how in the hell would your lawyer have the thought to include this in the documents, huh?"

Morgan glanced down at the page again, reading carefully. *Full custody is to be granted to the mother by the client forfeiting all biological paternal rights.*

Morgan's eyes broadened as she took in the significance of the sentence she had just read.

"You know what that means?" Jarvis antagonized. "I'll tell you. Claiming no rights as their biological father essentially makes it necessary to claim parental rights in the first place. Did you think of that? My lawyer. The *family* lawyer who has dealt with this and every other legal action my family has ever had needs me to now prove I have paternal rights so I can therefore forfeit them. How messed up is that?"

Morgan found her way to a stool and sat, clasping one hand over her mouth.

"And now they know," she whispered.

"Don't act surprised," Jarvis tapered his gaze, fixating on Morgan, inching closer to her after keeping the countertop distance between them for most of the exchange. But he couldn't help noticing that Morgan didn't flinch. The closer he got, the more she straightened her pose.

"I wasn't the first was I?" she asked.

"What are you talking about?" Jarvis quipped, confused by her reaction.

"You know, with me... I wasn't the first 'indiscretion' Emily and the family lawyers had to fix, am I?" She irately flung air

quotes up with her fingers before continuing. "They probably told you to shape up because they weren't going to bail
you out again, right? So, when you found yourself doing
the same thing, taking advantage of a drunk girl at the frat
house— again—you thought you'd cover your tracks. Make
sure I never said a word to anyone. And then when I got pregnant... You never expected that, did you? They weren't gonna
fix that, were they? Or was this never-claim-them-as-yours
thing all your mom's idea?"

Jarvis stepped closer, lowering his mouth to her ear and
hovering over Morgan as she sat cool as a cucumber with her
back resting on the countertop stool. "You don't know what
you're getting yourself into," he muttered into her ear.

Pushing herself back in a quick scoot, she hopped down
from the seat, standing to look him squarely in the eye.

"How many were there after me, Jarvis? Before me? Did
you have to pay them off too? Did momma help you with any
of those?"

"You don't know anything. You'd better watch it. I will
bury you! You'll get nothing!" Jarvis argued, speaking more
loudly with each proclamation.

"Keep it all, Jarvis. I don't need anything from you. The
only thing I care about is my kids. *My* kids," she cried, pounding a finger to her chest. "You let me know how you felt about

them a long time ago, and I'm not about to let you continue to bulldoze my life. Get. Out."

Morgan decisively reached her hands upward, shoving Jarvis' chest, allowing herself to finally push back. Literally.

Jarvis rapidly clasped his hands tightly around her wrists, flinging her to the ground. After hearing the loud thump from their mother's body hitting the laminate floor, Milo and Sadie rushed out of the bedroom.

"Dad, please," they shouted in nearly perfect unison. "Please don't!"

"Kids, go to your room. Your mother pushed me and I simply pushed back." Jarvis said, his hands raised high in the air. "I'm leaving. See?" he said as he was backing up toward the apartment entrance. "Now, go back into your bedroom."

"It's fine," Morgan added, lifting herself from the floor. She had managed to crawl to the living room, just behind an end table that provided a tiny bit of protection, should Jarvis decide to lunge at her.

"I'm okay," she waved her hands as if to demonstrate that she was fully mobile. "Your dad and I will work this out. It's just legal stuff and it can get heated," Morgan managed a deep breath and a nod toward her children.

"You sure, Mom?" Milo said through tears.

Ever since he'd spent time away, engaging with his feelings, it was as if Milo was learning a new version of himself. One that wore feelings on his sleeves and expressed exactly what he meant when he spoke. He battled more with finding a balance between what others had the right to know about him and how to express his innermost thoughts than with his ability to reveal hidden emotions. Every sensitivity he possessed seemed to dance atop his skin, exposed and ready to pounce.

"Yeah, it's okay, baby. I'm okay. I promise." Morgan met his intense gaze and nodded her head, motioning toward the bedroom. "Sadie, take your brother's hand. Both of you, try to rest. I'll be in there in a second, okay? Your dad's just leaving now," she announced.

Milo quickly shifted his stare to his father as Sadie, speechless, began tugging on his arm.

"Yeah, your mom is right. I'll go," Jarvis confirmed. He backed up, extending his hand toward the doorknob as the twins reached the door to the bedroom, closing it tightly before leaning their ears against the wooden surface.

"What have you done to him?" Jarvis quietly asked Morgan once he thought Milo was out of earshot. "You've messed everything up, haven't you?" he said under his breath, wagging his head before turning the handle. "You're ruining them."

Morgan stood silently, waiting for Jarvis to exit, standing unmoved. "You can leave now. Get out," she repeated.

As the door creaked open, allowing just enough space for Jarvis to step outside, Morgan rushed to the doorway, pushing it closed, and clasping the latch behind him. She fell to her knees and began to weep as the twins hurried out into the living room.

"Is he gone?" Sadie asked as she lifted herself onto her toes, glancing through the peephole. She was unable to see anything past the hallway that connected their entrance to the outdoors.

"How did he even get in the first door?" she asked.

"That's a good question," Milo said, offering his mother a hand, and helping her to her feet.

"It's your dad," she shrugged, pulling them both in for a hug. "He's got a way of knowing stuff. But we're okay. It's going to be okay. Let's just go back to bed."

"What?" Sadie was befuddled. "Who can sleep?" she asked.

"Not me," Milo agreed.

"I mean, just come into my room. We can watch a movie," Morgan smiled.

"Ooh, I'll grab extra blankets," Sadie agreed.

"Nice. I'll make the popcorn," Milo said.

"At 6 a.m.?" Morgan grumbled.

"Mom, we just witnessed the aggressive actions of our lunatic father. We earned popcorn," Sadie declared matter-of-factly.

Morgan grinned, despite feeling overwhelming grief at the truth of her daughter's statement. Without exchanging another word, the family unit of three piled onto the comfortable king-size bed, turned on a movie, and munched popcorn.

Chapter 12
Holding On

During the tawny morning hours of a chilly autumn weekend, Milo and Sadie took the forty-five-minute drive to work with their mother, watching the sun peek over the horizon, making the distance from town to city seem small. They spoke to each other in whispers, as if they could push the flaxen light away with just a breath. Perhaps it was because their world had recently flipped upside down that allowed the twins to appreciate the smallest beauties in life, but Morgan knew the depths of what the season meant to the three of them.

Autumn had always been their era of freedom. From the moment Milo and Sadie were old enough to walk, as the leaves began to change, Morgan would take them on long drives, descending into protected trails of the national forests. It was sacred to them. They would each collect their favorite leaves, acorns, pine cones, and rocks. A large bowl on the dining table cocooned their treasures as they methodically organized their trinkets, forming a display that all of them were proud of. The reverence they felt for the golden memories they built together each fall was understood, never spoken. They let the peachy light caress their skin in silence. Soon they'd be part of the organized chaos that is a Sunday morning brunch at the most popular place in town.

Timothy Foleson and his business partner, Jessica Whitaker, had empowered Morgan to use her budding IT skills to set up the restaurant's entire workflow, with the expert help of the salesperson who had sold them the operating system. The software had been Morgan's idea. She researched platforms and found one that, while backed by a newer company, offered far more features. Morgan was truly tapping into her strengths even after years away from the secular workforce. Pouring her heart and soul into restaurant management allowed Timothy and Jessica to focus on their culinary expertise. Each menu option was planned with meticulous care. Since Morgan had stepped in, the bistro had run seamlessly and had more patronage than they could have hoped for. Things were going so well, the partners were already starting to look for a new space to expand their business.

Morgan restricted online booking to two months at a time, and people were lucky to find a table if they didn't grab a reservation within the first forty-eight hours it went live. Patrons relied on their phone notifications to alert them when new listings opened up and scheduled their recreational time accordingly. Some people complained about not being able to get a table, but the new entrepreneurs considered that to be a wonderful problem to have.

Morgan drank in the bumbling sounds of a fully operating restaurant, feeling invigorated after a meager five hours of sleep. She patrolled the floor, looking for any deficiency she might address for employees. No job was too big or too small for Morgan, and the restaurant staff couldn't imagine having a better leader.

"Mom, can I just sit at the bar for a while?" Sadie approached the patio entrance where Morgan was about to clear off a table.

"Is there a seat?" she asked. "You know this is our busiest time of the week."

Sadie nodded, with a fretful look on her face.

"What's going on?" Morgan pulled her daughter into a corner tucked between the indoor and outdoor spaces where servers would stash clean silverware and extra menus. "You okay?" she lowered her voice.

"Aimee just walked in with some of her friends. I was taking pictures of a couple of place settings from the fall menu, and..." Sadie didn't finish her thought.

"Aimee Scott?" Morgan asked breathlessly.

Sadie nodded again.

"Okay, do you want to go in the back? You could help your brother wash dishes," she winked. Morgan tried to lighten the tone.

The twins had been offered a few hours of work at the restaurant every weekend. It was an added relief to Morgan that they had their own spending money, even though she knew it was less than they'd been used to having at their disposal. Jarvis hadn't been extravagant with them, but he had been more generous with their allowances than he had with hers.

The truth was, if she wanted to, Morgan could still go in and transfer money from the kids' savings; she still had access to their accounts. However, since nothing had been settled through the divorce lawyers, she was advised not to generate any activity in the bank accounts.

Milo spent most of his time as a dishwasher and was occasionally asked to bus tables when things backed up. Sadie did every setup job you could think of. From wrapping cloth napkins around the chunky silverware to sanitizing menus after each use, Sadie's hands were always busy. With her artistic flare, it wasn't surprising that she had a knack for photography, and she quickly became the go-to gal for the bistro's social media content. The one place she didn't love in the restaurant was the kitchen.

"No, Mom, please. I have these posts to work on." Sadie tipped her screen toward her mother, and Morgan watched moving images dance in slow motion. A champagne flute sparkled with exploding bursts of carbonation while to the side, a fluffy omelet was being carefully folded onto a plate.

"Gosh you're good at that," Morgan beamed. "That's gorgeous. Okay, go finish your work. I'll make sure Aimee and her friends sit outside. It's lovely out there with the heaters on. You know you'll have to give up the seat at the bar if we need it, right?"

Sadie gave her mom a look that assured her she understood.

"It's the only spot we have for walk-ins, poor souls. They just keep showing up," Morgan grinned. She gently leaned in to kiss her daughter's flawless skin.

"Thanks, Mom," Sadie said sincerely as she returned the gesture, brushing her lips against her mother's cheek. She felt a wave of gratitude threaten to spring up in a gushing flow of tears, and instead of giving way to the sensation, hugged Morgan's waist tightly. "Really, thank you, for everything."

Morgan smiled compassionately, making her way to the front of the restaurant as Sadie headed in the opposite direction, luckily finding a couple of empty stools at the end of the bar. Sadie let out a deep sigh.

"Hey, what's up lady?" the friendly bartender, Melissa, asked. "I know you had a birthday recently, but I'm not sure

I can legally serve you what I've got stashed back here," she teased.

It was exactly the lighthearted greeting Sadie needed to fully suppress the fear that struck her when she saw Aimee walking into the bistro.

"You know," Sadie began to explain, "in some places in the world, I'd be allowed to order a mimosa instead of just taking photos of them."

"Well, not in this jurisdiction, I'm afraid," Melissa replied, scooting a bowl of hand-rolled bar pretzels toward Sadie. "But I *can* get you some orange juice."

"Perfect," Sadie grinned, placing her phone on the bartop and exploring the font selection for an Instagram reel she had been working on. As she reached for her earbuds, about to listen to music, two walk-ins arrived at the bar and asked everyone to accommodate their desire to sit next to each other. The two barstools right next to Sadie were made available for the newcomers and she shifted to ensure she didn't take up more space than needed. Sadie was almost grateful they had come. If anyone glanced over at the bar, they would see it was full. She would now likely be able to sit there for an hour or more.

"I seriously can't believe that's Aimee Scott," the woman one seat over began. "What are the odds?"

"I know," the woman sitting next to Sadie replied incredulously.

Sadie couldn't have agreed more. What *were* the odds? There was no way she was putting her earbuds in now.

"Do you think she saw you?" the one next to Sadie continued.

"Who knows?" the first woman said. "She barely noticed me in the three and half years I worked for her! Can we get two of your bottomless mimosas?" she asked before Melissa had a chance to interrupt the young women's exchange.

"Coming right up," Melissa replied, winking at Sadie as she turned. Sadie looked down, desperately hoping the women didn't know she was eavesdropping.

"You know she's divorcing her husband, right?"

"What?" the former employee exclaimed. "Well, I never thought we'd see the day!"

"Really?" her friend scoffed cynically.

"Yeah, I mean, she has been having an affair with the other guy for probably a decade, so what gives now?"

Sadie's eyes widened as she sucked in a sharp inhale, lowering her head further. She kept an elbow on the counter, resting her head in one hand while tapping her screen with the other, pretending to work.

"Do you think it's true? I mean, we all know that little town has a reputation for oddities, but would the eye doctors who plaster their faces everywhere together be so bold as to hide in plain sight?" the woman tittered.

"Yep. I *absolutely* think so," the woman nodded. "Everyone talks about Dr. Connor being a player, but he's more of just a clueless, arrogant flirt. At least, that's what I saw. I didn't work in the main office, and everyone talked about him and Vanessa, or whoever the girl was before her, but I *always* saw him with Aimee," she explained, emphasizing the word *always* as if it were the only one that mattered in her announcement.

"So, I guess if they're both divorced, that means they can be together. After all that time," the friend said. "My, my, my," she added before raising a glass to her lips.

Sadie wanted to melt right there in her seat.

"Do you think Dad and Aimee are having an affair?" Sadie whispered as she crawled under the covers on the couch, curling her toes under her brother's leg to warm her feet from walking barefoot on the chilly hardwood.

Milo and Sadie had developed a routine in the 900-square-foot apartment. On Sunday evenings, after eating at the bistro, the Connor trio would drive home. Morgan would immediately shower and crash into bed, while the twins would pile extra blankets on the couch, make popcorn and pizza rolls, and watch their favorite shows together.

There was something about being a twin. Milo and Sadie could tire of everyone else and occasionally claimed that they had reached their limit with each other. But when push came to shove, there was nothing more comforting than resting their head on the other's shoulder, the one person they couldn't imagine living without. Closeness wasn't a luxury to them, it was oxygen.

"Is it an affair when you're divorced?" Milo wore his pragmatic outlook on life like a layer of skin. Not like some who threw logic on like a cozy sweater. For Milo, no situation in life could be looked at without a clear assessment of the facts.

"Well, technically, they aren't divorced because nothing is final. And I mean, like, do you think they've been having an affair for a while?"

Milo put the bowl of popcorn on the coffee table in front of him, removing his heels from their resting place. Planting his feet on the floor, he looked his sister in the eye.

"Sadie, I don't know anything anymore," he admitted.

"Hey, I didn't mean to upset you." She paused. Sadie's fear for Milo permeated the air. She worried about breathing a word—the wrong word—and plunging him into the darkness that threatened to undo him just weeks earlier.

It was different for Milo, though. He felt as if a hinge had come unlatched. Shadows had relinquished their hold on this mind, opening him wide, allowing light to flood in. Not that the darkness wasn't there. But it remained beneath the soles of his feet as he trampled above ground, a clear distinction between where the shroud of pain belonged and what walking in gratitude can feel like. He wasn't sure that he would always be able to evaluate his life in that same way, but he was willing to make the firm choice to live and find a reason to do so. Every day. He couldn't blame those he loved most for wondering at his sudden change. Even though they knew him to make up his mind and stick to his decisions, it would take time. For all of them.

"God, Sadie, you don't have to worry about upsetting me. You of all people. Isn't this whole thing upsetting? Like, how am I supposed to react?"

Sadie sighed. "Yep. It's the worst," she confirmed. "But I heard some women at the bar today talking about Dad and Aimee. And, I just... I don't know. It's so annoying that Mom gets all the shade thrown her way, and Dad is just the guy everybody thinks is funny and smart, and oh, by the way, has a reputation for being a flirt or a cheater. Whatever, no big deal. But when Mom is accused, it's a fight. Divorce, but not a divorce because she doesn't deserve his money. And also no one should help her because a woman who cheats, well, that's unacceptable. Anyway. It's just not fair."

There was a halt in the conversation, allowing the siblings to absorb the weightiness of Sadie's thoughts. She tucked her arms securely under the blankets, pulling an edge to her chin, and sank as low as the plush fabric would allow.

"Do you think Mom cheated?" Milo finally asked.

"Probably not," Sadie hypothesized. "But honestly, I wish she would have. It would have made things easier."

Milo's eyes expanded. "What? How do you figure?"

"At least she'd be gettin' some," Sadie tilted herself forward and grabbed the popcorn from the table. Cradling it in her lap, she rested her back on the couch. "And I hear *that* makes you happier," she smiled slyly.

"Oh my God, Sadie, seriously? Gross. You cannot joke about Mom and Dad's sex life with me. I can't handle it," Milo said. "I'm fragile, remember?" he teased.

Sadie rolled her eyes, lifting her heels above the cushions, and shoved Milo with enough force to tip him into the arm of the sofa, even though he saw it coming.

"I *will* tickle you," he told his sister, knowing that was the one thing that would immobilize her in one split second.

Sadie threw her hands in the air in surrender, repeating, "Truce, truce, truce."

And they leaned into each other, smiling, knowing there was one person in the world who would always feel like home.

Weeks passed like a rushing locomotive. That's the only way Morgan could describe it. She and Tiffany had gone to Europe together the summer between high school and college, and ever since their three-week tour on trains and boats across eight countries, she had a fascination with the mode of transportation that seemed to have been abolished from American life.

"Like a freight train," she told Tiffany, leaning over the bar.

"That's what you always say," Tiffany quipped.

"And it's always true," Morgan smiled.

"Well, I'm just happy to have a chance to come during the week so I can actually get a seat in this joint. Because your train doesn't make many stops in my neighborhood anymore," Tiffany joked. "Now, I gotta come to yours."

"I *live* in your neighborhood, Tiff," Morgan reminded her.

"I'm just goin' with the metaphor, Mo," she laughed. "You could say we're ships passing in the night."

Morgan chuckled, delighted to have her best friend at the counter. On a Thursday afternoon, the café wasn't empty, but there was enough of a lull that Morgan could chat between duties. She tapped the countertop with her hand and said, "I'll be back. I should probably check on things."

For the colder months, the restaurant had decided to invest in the courtyard, adding heaters and a metal structure with window panes that folded in and out like an accordion. After attempting to find an affordable larger space, Timothy and Jessica had decided to make do with what they had and continue through the winter in their current space instead of attempting to break their lease simply to keep up with demands. They had been allotted an extra 2,000 square feet of outdoor space in the city complex and weren't about to forfeit an inch for any season. Voluminous potted plants made the covered patio look and feel like a greenhouse, with tables set for parties of two and four perfectly situated between the vegetation.

As Morgan made her way through different seating zones, turning the corner and passing her favorite hibiscus tree, she felt her heart leap into her throat. She immediately rotated her body in the opposite direction and made a beeline to the bar.

"He's in the garden," Morgan said nervously.

Tiffany swiveled her stool. "What? Jarvis?" She recognized the look on her best friend's face, and there was only one person in the world who could evoke it. Morgan speechlessly nodded her head. "Did he see you? Does he *know* you work here?" Tiffany asked, befuddled.

Before Morgan could answer, she caught a glimpse of an employee walking Aimee toward the garden patio. She swung herself around to keep her back to Aimee, hoping to remain unseen.

"Ugh, Aimee was in here a few weeks ago with some friends. I guess she told Jarvis about it." Her tone deepened with chagrin. "My lawyer told me to have no interaction with him. This is just awkward."

"So, he's *not* stalking you?" Tiffany said skeptically. "And he hasn't been in before?"

Morgan chuckled. "No. I'm fine. I'm not afraid that he's gonna hurt me, Tiff. The only time he got physical was at the apartment. And I *did* push him first." She lightheartedly excused the behavior of a man who, whether or not she wanted to admit it, still possessed a certain hold on her emotions.

Morgan would often cry herself to sleep at night, missing him, wishing there was a way she could have pleased him during their lives together. Guilt-ridden, she'd awaken from her dreams where Jarvis had bought her flowers—something he did often in their marriage, a gesture he'd brag about to her and others, proving he was an attentive husband. In her dreams, as she took the bouquet in her hands and leaned up to kiss him, the petals would disintegrate between her fingers.

Then he'd twist his face, refuse her affection, and walk away. When she found herself awake in tears, she mentally beat herself up, wishing that she could somehow let go of giving even the tiniest shit about him. Morgan would let the regret wash over her entire being until she focused on morphing her attachment into hatred. Though she tried not to go there.

"Don't do that," Tiffany scolded. "Don't let him off the hook like that."

Morgan inhaled through her nose and blew out as if through a tiny straw.

"No excuses. But, really. I'm okay," she winked.

By the time her shift was over, Morgan had caught Jarvis' inadvertent glance as she moved past the bar and into the garden patio. It was clear that he had not planned the chance meeting. A flash of surprise eclipsed his face for a brief moment before he tightened his mouth with a smirk. He tilted his head in her direction, attempting to intimidate her, but Morgan squared her shoulders, even though she felt her knees go weak.

Chapter 13
Letting Go

The basketball court smelled of sweaty high schoolers, sneakers, and industrial floor cleaning products. People crammed themselves onto the bleachers that were stacked only four rows high. St. Clair wasn't a basketball town—they ate, drank, and slept football—but the faithful fans of Spartan basketball were starting to grow in number. Since Coach Foleson had become the Athletic Director, he had put more and more emphasis on broadening students' options. He had rented a pool in town at the recreational complex facility to start an official swim team only two years earlier and had added baseball and soccer. This year: basketball. The one wooden-floored gym at the end of the school property was smaller than the football team's weight room, but they made due. Every time they'd host a new school on their premises, the team would walk in, take one look around, and assume they'd wipe the floor with the meager small-town boys. And after every game, the opposing team's players would leave surprised and a little embarrassed. St. Clair High basketball was officially undefeated.

Morgan hadn't been able to make it to any games since Milo joined the team, but she was thrilled that after giving up swimming, he joined both the theater program and basketball for his extracurriculars. Keeping him busy took a load of worry off of Morgan's shoulders.

Since he was new to the sport, not to mention most players towered over him, Milo mostly sat on the bench, but it was the atmosphere of a team sport that he loved. He needed that camaraderie in his life, the assurance that those pushing towards a common goal would relentlessly look out for each other. Like a flock of birds that effortlessly pendulate in harmony, intent on safely reaching their destination together. Milo might not have realized that it was one of the things that kept him above the murky depression that sometimes beckoned him, but Morgan did.

She tiptoed her way through a few of the parents and student supporters to find Sadie.

"Hey, Mom!" Sadie said cheerfully. "You remember Kaitlin?"

"Oh, hi, Kaitlin. It's been a while," she smiled.

"Yeah, it has. Nice to see you again, Mrs. Connor" Kaitlin said.

"Oh, just call me Morgan, please," Morgan insisted.

When Kaitlin gave her a silent stare, looking befuddled at the notion of calling her friend's mom by her first name, Sadie nudged her with a giggle. "She's getting a divorce and no one knows what to call her," Sadie explained flippantly. "Just call her Morgan, it's fine."

Morgan grinned, happy to be in public, visibly thriving alongside her children and feeling a celebratory atmosphere. She was proud of herself and her kids for making it through the hardest time of their lives. Even though the divorce seemed to be taking an eternity, there was hope, and a sense of moving on, even if the documentation didn't substantiate it.

Morgan's sense of calm dropped to the floor with a plunk as she witnessed Jarvis entering the side door of the gym.

"You didn't tell me that your dad comes to these," Morgan said, leaning into Sadie's ear.

Jarvis had reached out to Milo, trying to rebuild what little relationship they had, expressing interest in having dinner or coming to Milo's swim meets. When he told his dad that he had quit the swim team, Jarvis added it to the list of reasons he believed Morgan was ruining their children. 'Connors don't quit' was a motto each of them was expected to maintain, and they knew it. Neither Morgan nor Sadie were aware if Milo was conversing with Jarvis regularly. The thought made both of them uneasy.

Making his way to a section of the bleachers that would give him a clear view not only of Morgan and Sadie but of the coach and players, Jarvis laid his jacket on the seat before sitting down.

"He doesn't come. Not usually. But I guess he heard Johnny is the new basketball coach and he's coming to spy on us all," Sadie ridiculed.

"What?" Morgan was genuinely shocked. "Johnny is the new coach?"

"You didn't know that?" Sadie asked.

"No," Morgan confirmed. "Why didn't Milo tell me?"

"Umm," Sadie began in her quintessentially sarcastic tone, "Probably because the guy that people accused you of having an affair with didn't move out and go back where he came from and instead got a desk job at a college. Then, to pick up extra cash, he had to coach a high school basketball team," she said in an exaggeratedly jaded tone. "So, he thought he'd skip telling you, Mom."

"Wow, you're pure joy and sunshine," Morgan said, wagging her head at Sadie.

"I'm here all night," Sadie chirped. And they both laughed, admiring each other's strength.

As the game commenced, Morgan and Sadie's enthusiasm grew while the teams squeaked their way up and down the court and the crowd became more and more spirited. The rush of adrenalin watching a bright orange basketball whirr through the air before the indelible swish of a three-pointer was intoxicating. Even though Milo only got to play for a few minutes at the end because one of the players fouled out, Morgan and Sadie beamed with pride.

"Hey, let's go get some ice cream and celebrate," Morgan suggested as she and Sadie met up with Milo in the hall.

"Mom, it's November. It's, like, already snowed. It's freezing," Sadie said.

"The snow melted!" Morgan reminded her. "And since when do we not eat ice cream in the wintertime?" she asked. "That never stopped us before!"

"I can't, Mom," Milo explained. "I'm goin' with the team anyway. We're gonna hang out with Coach. He's got snacks and stuff for us already. Can you pick me up later? I'm gonna ride with Jake and he has to leave early."

"Oh, so not at the Foleson's?" Morgan asked.

"No, Coach Barlow's house," Milo hesitated. "Is that okay?" He hadn't intentionally avoided telling his mom that his new coach was Johnny, but he did realize at the moment that she probably didn't have prior notice of it, and felt a pang of guilt.

"Yeah, I'll come by and get you later. Just text me. Have fun," Morgan said, nonchalantly, sensing her son's regret. "I'll be there by ten, okay?"

It was an interesting time of life for Morgan. The twins were technically old enough to drive a car, yet neither one of them seemed remotely interested in trying out their luck behind a wheel. Morgan assumed it was because they knew their dad wouldn't supply a vehicle for them unless they lived under his roof. And if they didn't have a car, they didn't need a license. She found herself often acting as a driver for two pretty grown-up individuals.

"I'm gonna go with Kaitlin, Mom," Sadie said as Milo walked toward Jake's car.

"Well, okay. I guess I'm flying solo tonight," Morgan replied. "I bet your Aunt Tiffany will eat ice cream with me," she joked.

"I bet she will," Sadie winked. "See you later okay?"

"You don't need a ride home?" Morgan asked.

"Nah, Kaitlin and I are gonna go to the diner and then she'll drop me off at home. I'll be back before you get Milo. I can ride with you if you want."

"Sounds good," Morgan replied.

Sadie and Morgan's relationship had blossomed into a friendship that Morgan nurtured judiciously. She wanted to maintain their closeness, and yet not have to rely on her six-teen-year-old for comfort and validation. But that goal was challenging to accomplish when the path she was traveling ended up crumbling beneath her feet.

As she stepped between her car and a pickup, the shadowy figure of her soon-to-be ex-husband was unmistakably moving toward her.

"What are you doing here, Jarvis?"

"I'm watching my son's basketball game," he responded.

"Not here at the game," Morgan clarified. "Here at my car. You shouldn't be here. Our lawyers can handle anything you want to discuss."

"So, that's how it's going to be?" he asked.

"That's how you've made it, Jarvis. I am not supposed to be talking to you," Morgan put her hand on the door handle and heard the car unlock.

She moved slightly, opening the door and shuffling her body to the side, trying to slip into the driver's seat before Jarvis could wedge his way in between the vehicles. But she wasn't quick enough. Jarvis caught the open door with his hand. He clasped the rim, holding on tightly. The two of them were wedged between her door and the massive truck. There was not enough room for her to shimmy her body into the car and avoid the confrontation altogether, but she kept her hand on the door next to Jarvis, just to prove she wasn't giving in.

"Jarvis, don't do this. Just sign the papers. I don't need your money," Morgan pleaded.

"Why, because your 'high school coach boyfriend' is gonna take care of you now?" he taunted.

"You don't scare me," Morgan lied.

"Your eyes tell a different story, don't they?" Jarvis chuckled, leaning in close enough for her to feel his breath on her skin.

"Please," she whispered. "Please just let me go."

"Change the damn papers, Morgan."

"They're your *kids,* Jarvis. Don't you care, even a little bit? You are asking me to alter paperwork that will practically guarantee you never take care of them long-term," Morgan rehashed. "I can't do that."

"What are you talking about?"

"I'm not stupid, Jarvis. If I sign this and, God forbid, something happens to me, they have nothing." Morgan met his caustic tone with a force.

"They have their trust funds," Jarvis blurted.

Morgan shook her head. "And they'd have no living family members but my mother and me. I can't do that to them. They need to decide for themselves if they want a relationship with you when they're of age. And if they don't get *you,* they at least deserve your money."

Jarvis felt his blood begin to boil. "You think you're so clever, don't you?" Jarvis roared, raising his voice enough to draw attention.

Spectators unhurriedly filed out of the school building towards their vehicles. People meandered, chatting and celebrating another victory. Morgan had found a spot for her SUV near the entrance, where it was now flanked by two large trucks, concealing her and the man who refused to relinquish his last bit of control over her.

"People will hear you," Morgan muttered. "You really want to do this?" she asked, fixating her gaze on Jarvis. "Because if you want to make it a scene, I will," she said, finding her resolve.

Morgan had moved her hands to the inside rim of the door, hoping to grasp it and force Jarvis backward. Before she could move, her hand slipped and Jarvis shoved her forward, plunging her body into the door, her right hand lodged between both rims. She yelped, falling to her knees.

"Hey, what's goin' on?" Anthony Clemmons, owner of the towering Dodge Ram next to her car, inquired as he approached. He had heard the commotion of Morgan's hand getting smashed in the door.

"Oh, hey, Jarvis," he paused, clearly recognizing the Connors. "Is everything all right?" Anthony asked as Jarvis forcefully took Morgan's elbow, yanking her to her feet.

She let out another agonizing cry.

"Ow!" Morgan howled, turning towards Anthony. She wanted to be sure he could witness exactly what was happening as more people began to gather, huddling around the back of the vehicles. "I'm asking him to leave," Morgan attested, raising her voice. "You just need to go!" she shouted, just short of a scream.

Backing away, Jarvis casually flung his hands upwards, "Fine, I'm going. I don't understand what you're so upset about, Morgan," he deflected, speaking more to the small crowd than to her, seeming completely unbothered by the whole thing.

Morgan let an animalistic cry escape her lips. "Whyyyyy??" she shrieked before agonizingly slipping into her car, closing the door behind her. She looked at her hand, shadows distorting her view in the dim lighting of the school parking lot. It was already swollen—probably not broken—she convinced herself. She felt hot tears streak her face as she pulled out of the parking lot and silently drove down the road toward the hospital.

"Mom!" Milo inadvertently grabbed his mother's arm. "What happened?"

The two of them had been the first ones up on Saturday, meeting each other in the kitchen. Milo prepared a bowl of cereal, a late morning breakfast on Morgan's only day off work that month.

"Easy!" Morgan said, pulling her hand close to her chest. "It's attached, you know."

"Oh, sorry! But what happened?"

"Relax, it's just a hand splint," Morgan tried to set her son's mind at ease.

"Okaayyy? Aaand…" Milo elongated the words as he spoke, expecting an explanation. It wasn't like his mother to be elusive. Not when it came to talking things out. Morgan was quite direct in her approach to parenting. She had poured her heart and soul into her kids, sharing ideologies, philosophies, and emotions.

"It was caught between… I hurt my wrist…." Morgan stammered.

She had experience excusing Jarvis' actions. But this was different. She could sense a shift, a realization on Jarvis' part that he was losing every last bit of control over her, sliver by sliver. It was as if when she finally stood up to him, they transitioned their relationship. They had moved past the psychological games and plunged into the physical. Her fear was different now.

"Mom," Milo sounded as if he was scolding her. "Did Dad do this to you? Is that why Aunt Tiffany came to pick me up last night, and you were asleep when I got in? He didn't leave the school right away, did he?" Milo shook his head. "And I blew him off."

"What do you mean, you blew him off?" Morgan asked.

"He caught me coming out of the locker room and asked me if I'd go get pizza with him, just to talk. When I told him no, he grabbed my arm and practically dragged me to a corner in the hallway. He yanked my ear close to his mouth and started scream-whispering how it was your fault that he hadn't been able to see us and how I'd regret this someday. Stuff about papers that you won't sign and money that is rightfully mine and not yours," Milo explained. "Honestly, I was just trying to hold still and let him do his thing while the guys all came out of the locker room because I didn't want to draw attention. So, I don't remember everything. But he didn't leave, did he? He waited for you." Milo didn't give her time to answer. "And he sent you to the hospital."

Morgan had driven to the hospital as soon as she left the school. She checked Tiffany's location on her phone and decided it would be the best course of action. The women had taken advantage of the shared location feature on their iPhones for years. Rather than using the feature to watch out for each other's safety, they normally used it for fun. Like showing up where the other was shopping with a surprise lunch invitation. Or checking to see if Tiffany was on a shift at the hospital so Morgan knew whether to call or just text.

It would sometimes backfire. For example, unbeknownst to them, the hospital had a signal-blocking service that would oddly land Tiffany's location in a nearby lake. However, they figured out how to overcome that particular obstacle pretty quickly and ever since used the convenient method of checking up on each other almost daily. It also broke them both of the habit of saying, "I'll be there in ten," without meaning it.

"Milo, honestly, it wasn't serious. It *was* an accident, but I had to go to the hospital just to see if it was broken. Aunt Tiff gave me some pain meds that must have been super strong because I was so drowsy by the time we got home, I had to sleep it off. When she brought me home and offered to get you, I took her up on it. Really, it's fine."

"Mom, c'mon," Sadie walked into the kitchen. "I was here, and I saw you. Just be honest. I can't believe you're covering for him."

Morgan rarely felt tag-teamed by her children, but that's exactly what they were doing.

"Guys, I'm trying to keep the peace and stand up for myself at the same time. Your dad has never acted this way-"

Sadie cut her off. "Because you've never stood up for yourself like this before. You've poked the bear. Or, at least, you stopped placating the bear."

Morgan dropped her head, looking at the bowl of cereal, a wave of sorrow crashing against her as she contemplated her choices. It was at that moment that she realized the control Jarvis had over her was contrived. The cage she had built to protect herself was of her own making, and she now held the key. Perhaps the choice to free herself didn't exist before when the pressures of the world and her domineering husband dictated that she remain bound, but it was there for the taking now. It was natural to lean into regret, wondering what life would have been like had she found the strength to defend herself as a younger woman. She wished that she could wrap her children up—swaddle them into the little cocoons she used to blanket them in as babies and protect them from ever realizing that the world is a complicated and sometimes dangerous place. Morgan squared her shoulders.

"I'll be okay. I have a plan," she told them. "I think your dad will go for it. And once things are settled, you both can start to rebuild a relationship with him if you want. I've never wanted to come between that," she said as tears began to trickle down her face.

Compassion eluded the twins as they watched their mother's tears. Hearing the word *relationship* made them bristle.

"Mom, how can you say that? You want us to have a *relationship* with him? I would think you want to protect us from him," Sadie let her anger spill out onto her mother. "All this time you knew he was claiming *not* to be our biological father, refusing to be listed as our father on official birth documents, and you let him. And still, you gave us his last name, you pretended all this time. For what?" Sadie contended. "For us to have a father? That didn't work out too well, did it?"

Morgan could understand the pain her children carried and how one word could steer a conversation in a different direction. "I'm sorry," she said. "I was young, and just went along with what I was told was my best option, Sadie. They all just made it seem so logical at the time. You know, we sat in that lawyer's office for a prenup-"

"You had a prenuptial agreement?" Milo interjected. "Of course you did," he threw his hands in the air, wagging his head in disgust.

"Milo, no one marries into the Connor family without one. And the lawyer explained that there was a trust in place for you kids already, so I didn't worry about it. I knew we'd be provided for, and I thought that's all I'd need, you know?" Morgan sighed. "I didn't realize the real cost of things."

"And now that you know he *is* our father and *your* rapist? What now? Does he even want anything to do with us? And why should we care about him?" Sadie snarled.

"You don't have to. But if you ever want to, I think that door should be open. Because I don't want my issues to be the thing that robs you two of what you deserve. I know he won't ever let the Connor fortune or his relationship with his mother be affected, but he does truly love you. I guess he may have known all along that he was your father. He won't hesitate to allow you kids to have your share, as long as I'm out of the picture..." Morgan's words trailed off.

"Mom," Sadie said hesitantly. "What exactly *is* your plan? Please don't tell me you're planning something stupid."

The lights of the parking lot illuminated icy crystals of fresh falling snow, flecks of light bouncing from flake to flake. Morgan loved the fall but there was something special about winter, snow coming fast but slowly blanketing a mundane world, ushering the town into a mystical realm. November had turned into December with a force. The first winter storm hit before Thanksgiving, for the first time in more than a decade. Most of the white had melted into slush after the initial snowfall, but subsequent flurries, day after day, had cloaked the world in a quilt of alabaster. Roads were regularly cleared and travel wasn't significantly affected, so Morgan made her way in and out of the city for work without a hitch.

The commute allowed her silent space to think and she had come to a decision. One her lawyer would unequivocally advise against. Morgan was resolved to approach Jarvis with her proposal and demand a legal separation, once and for all.

The only thing she needed was a few days off to take care of business.

Morgan approached her car after a truncated work shift. It was the weekend, meaning she rarely had a moment to get off her feet. But she was blessed with the best coworkers and trusted the closing crew to be on point, so she decided to hide out and work in the back office, placing orders for the next week. The bistro had been running low on supplies needed for seasonal specials because the holiday rush had hit them in mid-November. Everyone seemed to prematurely have the spirit of the season. Morgan couldn't blame them. The only enjoyable thing about the long winter months was the celebration of life and the light of the season.

Before the crew left, they tapped on the office door, letting Morgan know they were heading out and offering to help if there was anything else she needed. She was ready to leave soon too, but when she found herself alone in the space, she walked around for a few moments, admiring what they had all accomplished. Morgan drank in the smell of the bistro, caressing the surfaces of the tables. She ran her fingers along the marble and hardwood and sat in silence at the bar for a good half hour, enjoying the tiny bit of eggnog Jessica had left in the fridge, scrolling on her phone.

As she crossed the parking lot, she was momentarily distracted by the glistening beauty of the night before noticing a hazy silhouette standing by her car. She slipped a hand into her purse.

"Jarvis?" she whispered, befuddled. Morgan squared her shoulders with purpose and approached her car without losing momentum.

"What are you doing here?" she asked, close enough to her husband to see snowflakes collecting on his scarf and hat.

"You need to sign the papers," Jarvis said tenderly. It was a tone Morgan hadn't heard from him in years.

"What?" she replied, almost startled at the sound of his gentility.

"I need the divorce, Morgan. Please," he sounded sincere, and Morgan's heart softened.

"I am happy to give you a divorce, Jarvis. I don't need anything from you. All I want is the safety of our kids."

"Great, then just sign."

He handed her a thick yellow envelope he had been concealing under his jacket, protecting it from the snow.

"I am not going to just sign the papers you've been holding over me for months as-is, Jarvis. But if you don't want to legally grant me all parental rights, then I want to see the paperwork for the trusts. The ones we established when they were born. I want to be the sole trustee and have a guarantee that our kids will be taken care of. Surely that is enough to convince Emily that none of us will ever get a penny from your family other than what is in those accounts."

"So it *is* about the money," Jarvis scoffed. "You act all high and mighty as if you're better than the greedy upper class. But when push comes to shove, it's the only thing you care about." His eyes darkened. "You bitch," he said, no louder than a whisper. "I will rot in hell before I see you have access to *anything,*" he continued. He abruptly lunged at her, throwing the full weight of his body onto hers, and grabbed her throat.

Without thinking, Morgan pulled the trigger on the pocket pistol cradled between her fingers. A shot reverberated between their bodies. She hadn't even removed her hand from her purse. Time warped, distorting Jarvis' body as it fell cascading toward the ground. Morgan sidestepped, leaning herself against the car, and inadvertently lost the contents of her stomach onto the fresh snow. She stood up and surveyed the scene in disbelief. It was as if she was emptying herself of everything she knew to be true about herself before that very moment.

Chapter 14
Confession

Within minutes, the parking area behind Vivo Tower on Fifth Street was filled with ambulances and police cars. A fire engine blocked the entrance as passersby began to gather. Morgan remained mute as she was battered with questions, unable to lift her head.

No, no, no, she thought, holding her face in her hands, rocking herself back and forth on the ground.

"Mrs. Connor, we have to move you," an officer said.

Morgan had stumbled her way to the street lamp that had conjured a magical feeling of bliss just moments earlier. Resting her back on the concrete base, she was empty of logic. She couldn't respond, couldn't move, couldn't feel.

"I'm going to have Detective Stanton take your hand and put you in the car, okay, Mrs. Connor?" the officer continued to address her.

Detective Stanton was the kind of policewoman you'd expect to see on television. Her long wool coat brushed the snowy ground as she knelt in front of Morgan. She spoke in a low tone.

"Hey, there. My name is Cassie. Can I give you a hand?" She reached towards Morgan with a smile.

Her accent was slight, but she spoke like an out-of-towner, capturing Morgan's attention.

"You have an accent. Where did you live before you came here?" Morgan asked, lifting her eyes to meet Cassie's as if this was a social gathering. But Detective Stanton had worked with enough trauma victims to know that people react to trauma very differently, and a spark of connection had just appeared between them. She needed to snap Morgan back into her body, into the present, and ultimately, into the cop car.

"That obvious still, is it?" Detective Stanton grinned. "I grew up in Indonesia with an Australian mum and a Nepalese father. I've lived here for thirty years but I can't hide my roots."

"You shouldn't. Your accent is beautiful," Morgan assured her. Morgan extended her hand to allow Detective Stanton to help her to her feet.

"Just this way," Stanton directed. "Can I call you Morgan?"

"Yeah," she nodded in consent as they walked slowly to the vehicle. "Am I going to jail?" she asked.

"Well, I need you to wait in the car for now. You're practically soaked to the skin, so we'll warm you up and then have the medics come look at you. If they give us the all-clear, you'll come with me to the station, okay?"

Morgan didn't reply as she lowered herself into the back seat. After the detective closed the door, she took a good look at her hands. She wasn't holding anything. The police must have taken everything from her, including her purse, the gun, and her phone. As she began to process the realness of where she was, Morgan noticed blood spatter on her chest, puffer jacket, and hands.

"What have I done?" she began to audibly repeat as she waited, unable to break into sobs, but sucking air as if she'd been crying for an hour.

"Mrs. Connor?" a paramedic opened the door. "We're going to just take your vitals now. If you want to step out and have a seat right here in the back of the ambulance."

Morgan complied but had no cognitive understanding of what was happening. Not until she saw the ambulance fifty feet away, lifting a stretcher into the back, with Jarvis strapped into the gurney. Jarvis' hand slipped to the side and a paramedic quickly tucked it in. Blaring sirens began to squeal through the cold night air.

"I killed him," Morgan whispered to the young man taking her vitals. "I killed my husband," she cried fiery tears that pierced the skin on her ice-cold face.

The paramedic removed the stethoscope from her chest. "Ma'am it's best if you don't say anything right now. Do you have anyone you can call?"

"No," Morgan couldn't think straight.

"An attorney maybe?" the young man said.

"Oh, yeah. I do," Morgan replied.

"Okay, good. So maybe just ask about that when the officer comes back. You're in shock, but otherwise, you don't seem to have any injury."

The young man spoke slowly, articulating each word clearly.

"You'll need someone to help you through the process, though," he said, placing a blanket over her shoulders.

"I can't admit you to the hospital right now since everything seems to be normal, so the officers will take you with them. Okay? Do you understand?" he continued in a compassionate tone.

What Morgan could not have known at the moment was that the young man caring for her had helped his mother escape an abusive relationship less than a decade earlier. His stepfather had been a tyrannical authoritarian who manipulated and bullied him since the day he adopted him at the age of four. But it wasn't until he entered high school that his step-father began beating him—*like a man*—challenging him to fights and regularly denigrating him in public. When his mother saw that her son was in danger, it was the catalyst that afforded her the courage to finally escape their abuser.

But the thing he found excruciating to live with was the fact that they had left two step-siblings behind. They were barely in elementary school, but on the advice of counsel, who said his mother could be charged with kidnapping if she brought them with her, they abandoned the two sweetest children he'd ever known. He could only hope that someday when they were of age, his young siblings would forgive him for abandoning them. If they ever had a chance to reconnect. His stepfather still had restraining orders against both him and his mother. Suffice it to say, the young man's radar for knowing when a woman was in long-term distress was extremely accurate.

"Yeah, I understand," Morgan assured him.

"Detective?" The medic called Stanton over and gave the all-clear.

"Milo, we just need you to tell us everything that happened in the last twenty-four hours. Now, when was the last time you saw your mother?"

An officer sat across the table from Milo in an eight-by-ten-square-foot interrogation room at the police station. It wasn't like it is portrayed in the police shows Milo loved to watch. This room looked like a padded cell, barely large enough to seat three people around the cheap furniture.

"Um, I guess last night. After the Christmas show."

"Okay, what show is that?"

"The one at the community college," Milo answered as if the officer should know what he was talking about. When the officer stared at him blankly waiting for more information, he continued, *"The Christmas Carol.* It's a musical. My sister and I do junior community theater in St Clair."

"All right, and *then* what did you guys do?"

Milo shrugged. He was exhausted. As the blackness of night turned to morning, the little interrogation room offered no sense of reality, blocking out every sign of life but the two people present.

"We went out," Milo said. "It was our last performance. So, we drove around and looked at Christmas lights because that's just kind of a tradition after the Christmas show, and then the cast party was at the Johnson's house until, like, 2 a.m."

The officer leaned forward, inquisitively. "So, you're telling me a bunch of high school kids stayed at a party until 2 a.m. and everyone was cool with it?"

"Yeah, I mean, a lot of the parents are there too. They don't just leave us alone. It's like chaperone city," Milo exaggerated.

"Okay," the officer nodded. "So your mom went to the show, and then left for work? That's kind of a late night."

"Yeah, she works late most weekends. She came to the show and then went to the restaurant. I don't think she worked a whole shift, but that's kind of normal for her. She's the manager."

"And that's at bistr-oh day-lah-arte?" he asked, stumbling over the pronunciation.

"Mmm-hmm," Milo confirmed.

"So, that's why she leaves you alone late into the night most weekends?" the officer asked. "Because of her work there at the restaurant?"

"No, " Milo began. "It's not like that. She doesn't leave us alone. Aunt Tiffany lives upstairs, so we're not by ourselves. Can I see her now? Someone said that my mom's here too. I just want to see her," Milo said uneasily.

The officer rested his back against the chair, taking a breath before responding. "Well, we're just trying to find out why you kids just happened to come home...*at the same time* as your mother was shooting her husband in a parking lot." He emphasized his words, just in case Milo had any doubt of his meaning.

"Coincidence, I guess," Milo shrugged, trying to indicate that he was not going to be easily flustered.

"Okay," the officer pursed his lips, resting a hand on his chin. "Well, I'm sure the security footage will paint us a full picture," he said casually. "So, your sister said something about a plan?"

He steered the direction of the conversation to what he had already begun to suspect the story was, hoping that Milo would take the bait.

"A plan? No, she didn't, Sadie wouldn't have said that. Where is she?" Milo began to fidget in his seat, nearly standing at one point.

"Oh, take it easy, boy," the officer advised, reaching his hand across the table from Milo. "Just sit tight. When Officer Riley was in here with you, I was chatting with your sister, and now we're just swapping to see if the stories you tell will line up. You know, it's harder to keep a lie straight than the truth, Milo."

"I'm *not* lying," Milo claimed.

"So, you're saying there *was* no plan?" the officer persisted.

"No! I don't even know what you mean by that!" Milo said heatedly.

"Well, your sister told me that there was some sort of plan for your Mom to confront your dad about the divorce. Was that supposed to happen tonight?"

"No!" Milo shouted. "You're twisting her words. That's not what she said—I don't believe you. I know police are allowed to lie to people during investigations. So, you're not going to trick me," Milo announced, crossing his arms over his chest. "I want to see my sister. You can't make me stay here, right? I'm not under arrest?"

"Well, it's a little complicated," the officer said as he uncrossed his legs, placing his feet firmly on the ground and ensuring that his eyes were at the same level as Milo's. "You're a minor, and we can't exactly release you to a guardian currently, so you're going to be here for a while."

"I want to see my sister," Milo repeated. *"And* my lawyer," it finally dawned on him.

"Okay," the officer agreed, standing to exit. "I'll see what I can do."

The sun crept up over the horizon as its rays bounced off frosty terrain, blinding travelers on their journey. But the three Connors wouldn't have to worry about a commute. Not until after the sun had set on the longest day of their lives.

Shannon Townsley made her way into the holding room where Morgan was seated, dressed as if she was going to appear in court later in the day.

"Hey, Shannon," Morgan paused, confused at the sight of Shannon dressed to the nines. "It's Sunday, and I know you don't go to church," she chuckled. "Why are you so dressed up?"

"Ha, no. You're right about that," Shannon confirmed. "But I am speaking later at a summit for women in law," she explained with pride.

"Oh, I'm so sorry. I just didn't know who else to call."

"No, it's okay," Shannon flung her hand in a typical flowing gesture that made her ever-so-endearing.

Shannon talked with her hands as much as she did with her mouth. She was ironically known around the city courthouse as the court mime. She didn't mind the nickname and even played into it one year at the governor's ball when she wore a long black and white sequined gown with a matching mask. She didn't keep the mask on the whole evening, but she made sure to take advantage of every photo op she could with local officials before removing it.

"So, how long have you been here?" Shannon asked.

"I don't know. Since three or four, I guess." Morgan had no sense of time.

"Okay, why didn't they call me then? It's 8 a.m." Shannon was shocked that she wasn't the first call instead of the last. "You haven't told them anything have you?

"What do you mean? Tell them what, Shannon?" Morgan replied. "I shot my husband in a parking lot behind the restaurant. There's no investigation here," she said offhandedly.

Shannon threw her hands in the air, waving them from left to right. "Woah, woah, woah. Look, I'm a divorce lawyer," she explained. "We still have attorney-client privilege, but we'll need to see an expert about this, and you need to keep your lips zipped until that happens. I don't care *who* you're talking to."

"I don't need to talk to anyone else," Morgan explained. "I just want you here. You've been my fiercest advocate for six months. And I'm not about to try to convince someone else of anything. I just want you to tell me what I need to do next."

"Well, for starters, did they read you your rights?" Shannon asked.

"Yeah, I think so." Morgan attempted to remember the events of the past four-and-a-half hours.

"Okay, well, if they didn't, that would be amazing for us because they would have no right to keep you here if not."

"No." Morgan continued to search her mind for any indication that she wasn't trapped inside a ridiculously realistic nightmare. "They did. You mean an arrest, right?"

"Yes." Shannon nodded. "The only way they can keep you here is if they charge you. Otherwise, we walk out now and take you home to your kids."

"No." Morgan could hardly get out a whisper. "They're here."

Shannon stood frozen. "What do you mean? Your kids? What is going on?" she asked.

"I don't know," Morgan reiterated. "Everything's so messed up."

Shannon sat knee-to-knee with Morgan. "Look, I understand the need to not rehash history and the frustration of starting from scratch, but this is way beyond my pay grade. Let me call a friend of mine, okay? He *is* a murder lawyer and deals with cases like this all the time."

"You know I can't pay him, Shannon," Morgan said as the realization of that truth swept across Shannon's face. "The only reason you took my case is because you were going to be paid out of Jarvis's fortune. Plus, you felt sorry for me, so there's that." Morgan had a hard time keeping herself from being sarcastic in her bizarre state of confusion.

"Well, shit," Shannon said.

"Yeah, exactly. I need you, and I'm thinking you probably can't get rid of me now if you ever want to get paid. So, do you wanna take my case? You know if I win, we can get a settlement."

"It's not about the money, that's for sure," Shannon told her. "They're charging you with murder, Morgan."

"Yeah, because I killed him," Morgan repeated matter-of-factly.

"Okay, you've got to stop saying that. You defended yourself, and we're gonna prove it. Lord knows we have evidence."

As the sun settled lower and lower on the winter sky, a day that seemed never-ending finally began to show signs of bringing itself to a close, while Morgan, Sadie, and Milo—not yet allowed to be in the same room—tried to prepare themselves for the horrors they would soon face.

CHAPTER 15
JUDGMENT

HEADLINES OF SEVERE WEATHER ticker-taped across the screen as Morgan watched her mugshot go from large to small, remaining in the left corner of the television screen as a familiar reporter narrated a segment about the tragic shooting of a well-known and beloved doctor. She sat at her kitchen island, unable to grasp what the woman was saying. Her mind and ears heard nothing other than the sharp, shrill sounds of ringing.

"Can we turn that off?" Morgan asked as she drew a cup of coffee to her lips and proceeded to take a quiet sip.

"Oh, yeah. Sorry," Tiffany apologized as she walked to the coffee table, picked up a remote, and clicked the TV off. "Can I get you guys some more coffee?" she asked.

"Sure, I'll take a top off," Shannon replied before turning to Morgan again. "We have to keep up to date on what the public is seeing, so I do try to keep the news on. I know it's difficult, but the more we know, the better. For now, I will stay current on things and let you know the strategy as we go, okay?"

"Yeah, I get it," Morgan replied. "I just... I feel so hated. And I don't think any of this is going to be fair," she admitted hopelessly.

"It's hard to get a fair shake in the justice system, Morgan. And I won't ever play games with you. I have no experience whatsoever with criminal law. But I'm pretty well-known for being a pitbull in the courtroom. So, you can rest assured I'm going to do everything I can to get you exonerated."

Morgan nodded. She understood that Shannon was in over her head, but there was an unreasonable comfortability in knowing that this would be a first for both of them. As if some kind of beginner's luck was more worth betting on.

"So, let's go through some details," Shannon instructed. "I need to know everything that you would classify as abuse in your marriage, as well as details of when you did something that can be used against you. Our goal is to get your trial to another district, but this is going to be about money, not fairness. So, let's assume that we will not be granted that request."

Morgan let out a long sigh. "Okay."

"Who do you think you can name? You know, people who the prosecution could potentially convince to rally against you. I need a full list of everyone you can think of, and what they might say about you," Shannon asked.

"I don't know." Morgan's voice sounded weak and defeated.

"It's okay. We'll figure it out. But the more time we spend on this now, the fewer surprises we'll have to deal with later, all right?"

Tiffany leaned her elbows on the countertop. "I can help with this part," she said.

The women sat and exchanged information as they scrolled through Morgan's phone, thinking through ways of building a defense. Since Tiffany had bailed her out of jail, Morgan hadn't been doing more than sleeping and meeting with her lawyers. She was wearing an ankle bracelet that didn't fit in any of her boots. The winter days dragged on. It was as if an avalanche had buried Morgan's everyday life under the weight of its oppressive drifts.

"I think the biggest issue might be Emily," Morgan said. "She's got money to throw at this."

"Well, the good thing is that you're not fighting her," Shannon reminded Morgan. "You're not fighting Jarvis. You're not even fighting the state. You are only required to prove one thing—that you were defending yourself. Emily's money can't buy anything other than her hotel bill during this trial." Shannon winked.

Morgan wasn't quite convinced. There was a constant dread inside her that Milo and Sadie may be questioned further. Thinking that they might be forced to testify drove Morgan to a near-breaking point. As much as she didn't want to admit it, she had pulled her children into so many parts of her life that she had kept from them before. The twins understood that it was for Morgan's survival, but she didn't. To her, it meant she was cracking—disintegrating into bits and shards that could never be repaired. She kept attempting to find a spot for each piece, hoping to rebuild the mosaic that comprised the person she used to know. No metrics existed by which Morgan could score the chances of survival with her sanity intact, much less without additional trauma to her children. Who knew whether they were mature enough to handle this increasingly complex situation? Mom guilt took on new meaning.

She breathed in deeply and tried not to think about the worst.

Taking her seat behind a solid oak table, Morgan purposefully observed her surroundings. The courtroom wasn't like she had imagined it would be. A former church complex housed the current government buildings, and an old auditorium kept its familiar layout with the judge's desk at the front of the room, precisely where a pulpit used to stand. An elevated platform on a gradient with a large wooden encasement separated judge and jury from prosecutors, defendants, and lawyers, while lines of pews, divided by a center aisle, filled an area fit for a congregation—or the courtroom audience, in this case. Historic stained glass windows pillared the walls on either side. Every color of the rainbow danced across the room in quick flecks of light while people shifted and squirmed at the site of the accused entering. The court had granted Shannon's request for the trial to be held outside of St. Clair County, but because Madison was only two towns over, it didn't make a significant difference. A population who hadn't heard of Dr. Jarvis Connor was hard to come by.

Once Morgan decided to enter a plea of not guilty, the news had gone national. Every morning, there were reporters and locals alike who stood in line, hoping to gain entrance into the trial. The town of Madison hadn't seen crowds like this before, and they were ill-equipped to offer a holding room for an overflow audience. They had done their best to accommodate the buzz by setting up a television in the small dining hall on the property. Judge Katherine Richards, who had a reputation for being fair but lacking patience for courtroom antics, allowed cameras during the proceedings but forbade live streaming, so the people in the room were relied on to get the news out fast. Strangely, despite the attention the case received, it didn't quite seem like a media frenzy. There was a certain decorum and respect in the air, attributed to Judge Richard's reputation and the stern speech a county sheriff gave at the press conference announcing the trial would be held there.

In her opening statements, Shannon went into Morgan's history, providing ample evidence to back up her claims. Tiffany, Shannon, and Morgan had labored over those details for weeks.

Line by line, Shannon methodically told Morgan's story of suffering abuse at the hands of her late husband that, for many, was hard to fathom. Shannon held some of her cards closely, though. In her speech, there was no mention of the college rape, the neglect of their children, or any bright blue paint stains that marred Morgan's reputation. That would come later. For now, she was focused on revealing a pattern of behavior on Jarvis' part, the crux of Morgan's defense. They were hoping the big events that led them to their time in front of the judge and jury would play out like a cinematic courtroom drama.

If there was one thing Shannon was grateful for it was the fact that her request for a speedy trial was unlike anything she'd heard of in her years of practicing law. From arrest to the first day in court, only six weeks had passed. Shannon wondered if the swift turn of events was the prosecution's tactic to catch them before they were prepared, but she had become confident they would be able to prove Morgan had acted in self-defense. She was more than ready to present their case.

When the prosecution offered a plea deal, Morgan couldn't deny that it was tempting. She could accept the offer and try to hurl the horrifying events of her current life fully into the past, but the minimum prison sentence for voluntary manslaughter was ten years. And that was something she couldn't begin to fathom.

"But what if we lose?" she would constantly ask Shannon throughout their preparation.

Long evenings and early mornings had Morgan, Tiffany, and Shannon sleeping on couches and sharing Chinese food in the downtown office nearly every day.

"*We won't lose,*" Tiffany and Shannon would say in unison as if on repeat.

"We have the trump card, Morgan. We can prove this was self-defense," Shannon assured them. "You don't have to testify. I mean, you *shouldn't* testify. There's no telling how any of us come across on the stand, let alone while under this kind of stress. I won't even think of putting you up there. But we have enough evidence to show that you were battered and mistreated from the moment you met Jarvis."

So, there the women stood, fully prepared, yet at the mercy of the jurors, each with their own biases. Biases that would affect what they each heard, what evidence they'd believe, and how they would ultimately decide Morgan's fate. It was a terrifying realization, yet, it was the only choice Morgan had. She was throwing herself at the mercy of twelve perfect strangers.

"You will hear how Mrs. Connor *tricked* her husband into marriage with her pre-existing pregnancy. How she manipulated Dr. Jarvis Connor's finances in the early years of their marriage, to the point where Dr. Connor had to remove her from their joint account. How their separate finances placed a tremendous strain on their relationship, a continual burden that the deceased had to bear. We will show proof of Mrs. Connor's infidelity! And finally, we will show how, ultimately, just weeks before she cold-bloodedly murdered her own husband, Mrs. Connor had a raging outburst in the school parking lot, swearing that she would get her revenge," the district attorney bellowed.

Morgan's ears perked up. She had felt herself drifting during opening arguments, hardly able to focus on more than a few words at a time. But she had never said anything about revenge. At least, not that she could remember. It was a really good thing that the prosecution brought up the school parking lot incident because having the hospital records of her broken hand was a sound rebuttal. As she allowed herself to be more present in the room, trying to concentrate on the details of every incident the DA brought up, Morgan's confidence swelled. Perhaps Shannon was right.

Each morning of the trial, Morgan walked purposefully to the courthouse flanked by her two lawyers. Stoic, slow, and determined. She didn't know if it was because people believed her to be a stone-cold killer that an odd hush seemed to descend over the crowd when she appeared, but she was grateful that the frantic scenes she'd played out in her head didn't happen. Besides, nothing was like the reality of facing the possibility of life in prison.

"Can you tell us your name for the record?" the prosecuting attorney asked, as Morgan's eyes began to well with tears.

"Sadie Connor," Sadie said confidently, leaning into the small microphone secured to the wooden railing in front of the witness stand.

"Thank you, Ms. Connor, and you're the daughter of the defendant?"

"Yes," Sadie knew not to answer more than she needed to.

It surprised Morgan that, unlike the aesthetics of a courtroom, the cadence and syntax of this prosecuting lawyer seemed altogether familiar, solidifying her perception of what to expect in a courthouse drama. Marcus Bondar, a DA known for his flair, was quintessentially everything one would imagine a government employee on a quest for justice should be. Overly zealous about practically everything, it was his sincere belief that no matter the circumstance, when a person was killed, another should bear equitable culpability. His world was colored with black-and-white catalogs of infractions and correlating punishments.

"And you told police the night of the murder that your mother was planning something regarding your father? Could you state for the court what you meant by that, and perhaps, what the plan was?"

Sadie pushed herself to the back of the seat, allowing the hardwood to support her, and tapped into her sense of justice.

"The night of the *accident,*" Sadie emphasized her correction with a nod, "I told the officer that my mom was well on her way to sticking to her plan of ignoring my dad. Not that she had any other plans. And they twisted my words. She wanted out of the marriage, but she also wanted to make sure my brother and I were taken care of. That's all."

Morgan allowed the corners of her mouth to rise. The pride she felt in her daughter exceeded any fear she had of having the twins involved in the trial. For better or worse, she and her kids were in the thick of it together. One thing Morgan was grateful for was that Milo didn't appear on the witness list, likely because the DA's office assumed that a girl would be more vulnerable than a boy. And it came as no surprise to her that Sadie remained fierce, tenaciously testifying on behalf of her mother.

Over three days of trial, Morgan listened to opening statements from the opposing sides and four of the witnesses called by the prosecution, all while striving to remain stoic and unflappable. She knew there was a list of sixteen witnesses, and mustered the fortitude to persist in coming off as emotionless.

"And how would you describe the reputation that Mrs. Connor had in the community?" the DA asked yet another witness from their long roster.

"She was viewed as a good, respectable woman. A submissive wife and a good Christian," Anthony Clemmons replied. "But what you think you see isn't always the truth, you know?"

The prosecution had shown a snippet of video on the TV screen, revealing an ad that the church had run on Facebook Meta and other social media platforms featuring the Connors. The church ran special programs throughout the holidays geared toward young families. The ads showed real members of the church volunteering, performing, and promoting the activities that ran frequently during the season.

Morgan and Jarvis had been filmed years earlier, but the ads still circulated in all parts of the state, making their faces seem familiar to many in the area.

"So, when *this* took place," the DA flashed a photo of Jarvis' original social media post of the disparaging paint-stained driveway with the jarring words, *cheating wife*. Morgan hadn't seen the picture in nearly a year and squirmed in her seat, visibly bothered. "What were your feelings about that?" he continued.

"It was a shock," Anthony nodded.

"I can imagine," District Attorney Bondar acknowledged. "And there was a general understanding that this is what led to the divorce—Mrs. Connor's infidelity?"

"Yes. I mean, Pastor Johnny was let go because of it too, and then the next thing we knew, the Connors were gettin' a divorce," Anthony explained. "So, it just made sense."

"I see. And what did you witness in the school parking lot the night of November twenty-fourth?"

"Mrs. Connor lost it." Anthony wagged his head. "I dunno, Mr. Connor was, like, trying to talk to her and she just screamed. Kind of like a wild animal. I haven't ever heard anything like that except out huntin'," Anthony admitted.

"Hunting?" the DA questioned.

"Yeah," Anthony confirmed. "It was a squawk like the sound of an animal going down, you know? She was furious."

Shannon touched Morgan's hand. "It's all right," she wrote on a notepad in front of her. Shannon knew Anthony would be a hard witness to get through. It wasn't that Morgan didn't know the people in her hometown were judging her, but hearing from their mouths that they believed she could be a cold-blooded killer was jarring.

"Mr. Clemmons." Shannon began her cross-examination. "You described my client's screams as something you've only heard in nature, correct?"

"Yes," he replied.

"And would you say that Morgan's cry could have been described as responding to a threat? Perhaps calling out as a last-ditch effort to beg for her life rather than an angry outburst?" Shannon asked.

"Objection, Your Honor, calls for speculation," DA Marcus leaned into his microphone. "This is not an expert witness and cannot be relied on to give an opinion as to the nature of Mrs. Connor's outburst."

"Then I suggested the witness' testimony be stricken from the record," Shannon replied. "If he is not a reliable source as to the nature of what Mrs. Connor was going through, then why do we need his input at all?" Shannon shot back.

"Your Honor, may we approach?" District Attorney Bondar requested as Judge Richards waved the two lawyers forward.

The audience fidgeted in their seats and whispered to each other while the judge spoke with the lawyers. Shannon wanted Anthony's testimony stricken from the record. She knew he wouldn't be the only person to testify about Jarvis' stellar reputation, but she also knew that the more groundless testimony she could eliminate, the better her chances. As the two lawyers returned to their seats, the judge overruled the DA's objection and gave orders for a lunch recess. Morgan let out a sigh. She hadn't noticed how long she'd been holding her breath.

Emily Connor reminded most people of a movie star. Standing no more than five feet tall if she was lucky, her petite frame, smooth skin, perfect hair, and dazzling smile showed up great on film and she took advantage of it. She was the spokesperson for the famed Connor family, regularly showing up in magazines about Southern living and making TV appearances to discuss her philanthropy. The small town's reaction to her was opposite to their treatment of Morgan. They loved the Connor family matriarch. Swarming her as she walked into the buildings, reporters shouted questions like, "Are you testifying *against* your daughter-in-law?" and

"What are your comments on the guilt or innocence of Morgan?" Emily retained her decorum and said nothing other than "Good morning, hope y'all have a great day," and flashed her million-dollar smile.

"Mrs. Connor," the DA began.

"Please, call me Emily," she insisted.

"Okay, Emily," Marcus knew who he was dealing with, but even he couldn't have prepared for the amount of charm Emily exuded in public. He took a beat. "Can you tell us the nature of your relationship with your daughter-in-law?"

"Well, Morgan has always been...hard to read," Emily paused dramatically as if she hadn't precisely calculated every word she was going to say. "She doesn't have a very soft personality, so I can't say we've ever been close."

"And you objected to the marriage from the start?"

"I wouldn't say I objected. I just wanted my son to be happy, and I thought that he shouldn't be tied down to a woman who was already pregnant when they met."

"Gold," Shannon whispered to herself as the courtroom permeated with intermittent gasps. Once the claim was in evidence, the defense had free reign to argue their side of that story. And they were sitting on irrefutable documentation that Jarvis was not tricked into anything. Shannon let a confident breath escape her lips.

"So," the DA continued, "Would you say that their marriage was a happy one?"

"No," Emily replied.

"And you have, in fact, described Morgan as a gold digger?"

"I have. We are not unfamiliar with the type in our family," Emily smirked. She attempted not to sound smug, fully believing that she was capable of it but entirely unaware of how impossible it was for her.

"But Mrs. Connor signed a prenup, correct?"

"She did. So the only way that she'd have access to Jarvis' money is if he were dead," Emily explained.

"But not the family money?"

"No," Emily confirmed.

"So, why murder then?" the DA asked. "If she knew already that she'd never be able to touch the real fortune."

"Jarvis has done well on his own. I know that Morgan hasn't contributed to the household for years, and if he wasn't giving her what she wanted, I can only assume-"

"Objection," Shannon responded. "Your Honor, are we just making assumptions?"

"The witness is testifying to the likelihood of premeditation, Your Honor," the DA rebutted.

"Overruled," the judge agreed.

"You were saying?" the DA prompted Emily to continue.

"Well, I assumed that since Jarvis had to separate their finances years ago, she was more and more desperate for money. And that makes people do things you wouldn't expect."

"And the kids? How is your relationship with your grandkids?"

Emily's demeanor changed. When a person genuinely lights up about an individual or a specific memory, it sometimes looks like a flash of magic. Something mystical happens to their countenance, and it seems as if they've stepped into a realm of wonder, if only for a split second. When that emotion is fabricated, it's as if one can witness the heavy stage curtain being tugged on by its ropes, unable to go up and down as quickly as the actor would like. Emily took a moment to shift in her seat.

"Well, you can imagine that I don't love the term *grandma,*" she quipped as a subtle laugh swept over the audience.

"I can. No one would peg you for being a grandmother," the DA agreed.

Emily had the time and resources to keep herself looking no older than forty-five, and even then, a very young forty-five. When she told people that her grown children had teenagers of their own, there was genuine disbelief every time.

"But, yes. My grandchildren, even though not biologically ours, were always loved and cared for." The heavy curtain was not quick enough for this act. No matter how hard Emily tried, an edge of disdain in her voice betrayed her words.

"And they had money in trusts?"

"Yes. They will be taken care of."

"And the only person, then, who does not have financial security in the Connor family is Morgan, is that correct?"

"It is," Emily confirmed.

"Thank you," the DA replied.

"Mrs. Connor," Shannon began, "Or would you like me to call you Emily as well?"

"Please," Emily nodded.

"Emily, you said that your grandchildren, Milo and Sadie, have trusts set up in their names?"

"I did."

"And is your daughter-in-law listed as a trustee on those?"

"She is."

"So, she doesn't exactly need to kill anyone to get money, does she?"

"Well, my son was also a trustee, so she'd need cooperation, at the very least. And I doubt she was getting that," Emily explained.

"Okay. And you said that the reason things were set up this way is because you knew your grandchildren weren't biologically yours?"

"Yes."

"And your son knew that as well?"

"Yes. They don't even have a father listed on their birth certificates," Emily confirmed.

"Thanks to you?" Shannon asked.

Emily didn't respond. She recognized the tenacity in Shannon's personality, but she wasn't quite prepared for it.

"You were the one who told your son not to put his name on his children's birth certificates, is that right?"

Emily took in a short breath through her nose. "I was. I have been managing the money in our family for years. I knew that if we set up a trust when the children were born, we could make sure they were taken care of and the family assets would stay in the family, as it's been for more than a century."

"And that's important to you?" Shannon prodded.

"Of course," Emily said, squaring her shoulders.

"But, you weren't concerned that your son was marrying someone who was pregnant by someone else? Just that he wouldn't put his name on legal documents?"

"Well, of course, it was a concern," Emily admitted. "But when your children are adults, you can advise, not force."

"That doesn't seem to be true when there's a lot of money involved, though," Shannon insisted. "You have your ways of getting what you want if you're controlling the purse strings, don't you?"

"Like I said, Jarvis did fine on his own," Sally reiterated.

"But not at that time, right? You supported him through college, but he let you down, didn't he? Getting in trouble, then coming home with a pregnant girlfriend who he said was raped in college?"

Emily was more uneasy with every moment, but she only slowed her speech and turned up her smile.

"That was the story, yes," she confirmed.

"But you didn't believe it?"

"I did not," Emily admitted. "I don't know what kind of savior complex my son had and how Morgan got her hooks into him, but I thought she was a promiscuous girl who found her chance to rope in a big fish. And it worked."

"So, that explains your relationship with Morgan throughout the years," Shannon stated.

"I suppose," Emily conceded.

"And why you've never felt close to your grandchildren?"

"Possibly." Emily didn't want to give Shannon an inch.

"Okay, and were you aware that your granddaughter, Sadie, took a DNA test this year?"

There was no veil to mask Emily's face, no way to hide her surprised reaction. She visibly swallowed hard.

"No," she retorted.

"Your Honor, we'd like to enter into evidence defense exhibit 13, a DNA test. It's Sadie's 23andme account, and the results are clear."

"Objection!" Marcus Bondar roared. "Your Honor, if there's going to be scientific evidence submitted, we insist that it be from a reputable source and *not* some website. And, this is entirely outside the scope."

"Your Honor, the prosecution is insisting that this was a murder for money. We're arguing self-defense because, after years of manipulation and control, Morgan found out her husband's dirty little secret. He was her college rapist and the biological father of their two children—a secret that Jarvis did not want getting out."

Shannon continued speaking over the strenuous objections of the prosecution until Judge Richards finally called out, "Overruled." The entire courtroom had frozen in stunned silence followed by a burst of whispers, watching the scene play out as if they were witnessing the filming of an epic drama.

CHAPTER 16
SALVATION

S NOW PLOWS HAD BEEN treating the roads almost daily for the duration of Morgan's trial. The famous groundhog Punxsutawney Phil had already assured superstitious believers that they had another six weeks of winter to endure, but the last day of closing arguments was the warmest it had been since October. The sun shone brightly, casting a blinding light over every ice-crystal surface as the thaw deepened, and hope sprung up alongside the thought of an emerging spring.

Morgan gripped Sadie and Milo's hands on either side of her as they walked silently toward the courthouse. At Morgan's request, the twins had not attended every day of the trial, but on this day, the final day before the jury began their deliberations, they insisted. It was the last thing she wanted—for her children to hear the nitty-gritty details of why she should or should not be sent away for murder—but she had enough respect for them both to leave the decision to them. She thought about what it meant to be a mother; and how much she had decided *for* her children instead of *with* them. Parents bring little humans into the world and make so many decisions that will alter the course of their futures, affecting the entire trajectory of their lives. Morgan was just glad her father was not alive to see her like this.

The courtroom buzzed with anticipation as she entered, taking a seat at the defendant's table, hands clasped tightly in her lap. Sadie and Milo sat directly behind Morgan in the gallery. Tiffany, Mrs. Radcliffe, Johnny, a few coworkers from the bistro, and Jenny Foleson braved the scrutiny of their fellow townsmen, flanking the twins on either side. The pews in the old courtroom were filled to the brim, whispers rippling through the crowd like a gathering storm as the weight of the trial hung heavy in the air, a palpable tension that seemed to abbreviate every breath.

Morgan's eyes flickered across the room before landing steadily beside her. She met her attorney's gaze and felt grateful. Shannon's unwavering support had been a shimmer of comfort in the darkness of uncertainty. Shannon squeezed her hand. The DA on the opposite side stood tall and resolute like a figure of authority primed to deliver judgment. Morgan felt his righteous indignation steadily aimed at her.

For days on end, the prosecution had laid out its case, presenting evidence of Jarvis' professional success and elevated standing in the community with surgical precision. As arguments were made, Morgan felt the weight of guilt pressing down upon her. Memories of Jarvis' abuse resurfaced like ghosts from the past, haunting her with their whispered accusations. She was a woman controlled, manipulated, coerced, and abused, but when all was said and done, most hadn't seen it, and she had pulled the trigger.

"You have to tell me *everything,*" Shannon admonished her client in private after a few days of testimony where a steady stream of townspeople were called as witnesses. "They've put your daughter on the stand! Every person they've questioned somehow gives Jarvis a pass, as if they think he is blameless for what he did all those years. As if you couldn't possibly fear for your life with him in the picture."

"I cost a man his life," Morgan sorrowfully uttered. "He's dead because of me."

"Morgan," Shannon whispered. She wasn't going to say it again. It was tiresome, reminding Morgan day after day that she shouldn't mention she killed Jarvis aloud, because the truth was, she had. "I'm not asking you to let go of the guilt you feel right now. You wouldn't be the woman I know if you didn't have an overwhelming sense of grief about this."

"But I hated him too," Morgan exclaimed. "I wanted him dead, and I did it. He sucked the life out of me for so long, Shannon. I didn't mean to do it, but I don't think I'm sorry

I did. I just feel guilty that I killed a man," Morgan blurted through heavy tears.

Shannon threw her arms around Morgan. "After what he did to you, every feeling you have is valid. Nothing you say here is wrong. I got you."

Morgan melted into Shannon's shoulders, feeling the weight of the admission rise from her chest. She lifted her head again, finally able to simultaneously hold the truth of so many things in her hands.

Shannon wanted to proceed with their time-constrained work, and when she too felt the burden rise from Morgan's body, lifting into the air, and allowing them both to take a deep breath, she continued. "So, let's tap into your sense of reason and push your guilt to the side, okay?" Shannon instructed. The witness today," she sneered.

"Ugh," Morgan sighed. "Triston Witt is an ass," she said.

"He may be, but he came across as a well-spoken person of influence. Please tell me that there's someone—anyone—who has your back. You worked with some of the people from church for over three years, right?"

"Yeah, but Jarvis volunteered there too, and I guess if they never really knew him, I can't be surprised they never really knew me. People see what they want to see most of the time," Morgan moaned.

"Is there anyone else we can call?"

"I don't know. I thought the rape would be pretty shocking and sway things in my direction."

"Of course it did! Why else would they add four new witnesses to their list? They saw the jury's reaction and knew things were leaning our way. But, you can never know exactly what people are thinking. I just feel like we're losing some of these jurors to the onslaught of Jarvis fans," Shannon said.

Perhaps the most profound cruelty of an abusive relationship is that the deepest hurts happen without witnesses, in the quiet, in the dark, in the unprovable private moments between two people.

"We have a forensic data analyst," Shannon continued. "We can put him on the stand and prove Jarvis' controlling nature through finances. Plus, we do have some damning emails, but I just don't know. We need to shatter the picture that the prosecution is painting," she said.

Regardless of their efforts, Morgan's fate would soon be in the hands of a jury.

As Judge Richards entered the room, everyone rose in a synchronized rhythm, as if in slow motion. There was a heaviness to the day that permeated the participants. As the judge took her seat, everyone followed, and an eerie hush filled the room. Most mornings, Judge Richards would flash a warm smile and greet the crowd with a hearty hello, followed by quick information about the day's proceedings. But this morning, the elongated silence made her deep sigh vibrate through the small microphone.

"Good morning," she finally began. "There's a common misconception about the justice system. Many seek certainty in situations that are, in fact, open to more than one interpretation. That's why the burden is on the prosecution to prove their case *beyond* a reasonable doubt. That's why both the prosecution and defense teams use logic and reason in their arguments—because we are all trying to make sense of unreasonable circumstances. But we also all know there's a lot of gray in life and a colorful spectrum of possible scenarios. Especially when we're trying to determine the guilt of someone who has caused harm to another."

The speech seemed almost ironic as the bright winter sun sent massive rays of light through the stained glass, casting a kaleidoscope of colors across the courtroom's reflective surfaces.

"That's why those of us responsible for meting justice look for corroboration. Evidence. We want irrefutable information. We want encrypted data that provides real, tangible proof of the accused's guilt or innocence and leaves no room for questions or interpretations. Last night, this type of exonerating evidence was provided. It is because of this fact that all charges against Ms. Morgan Connor were dropped this morning."

The courtroom erupted with chatter as Judge Richards leaned into the microphone.

"I call for order in the court," she said sternly as the crowd's reactions subsided. "District Attorney Bondar and I were recently presented with evidence clearing the accused. It is apparent to me that Ms. Connor did act in self-defense, and as a result, I see no further reason to consume additional resources to continue this trial. Ms. Connor, I am sorry for the time and distress this has caused you, and I wish you well in your future endeavors. I need to see both counsels in my chambers. The court is adjourned."

With that, she tapped her gavel to its wooden stand, rose to her feet, and left. The feverish uproar that followed was indicative of the shock felt by nearly everyone in the room, but Sadie and Milo remained unflustered. Milo took his sister's hand in his with a grin.

"Let's go," he said, as they walked to their mother, falling into her embrace.

"What is going on?" Morgan repeated again and again, taking them, her mom, Tiffany, and Shannon into her arms as she wept.

It wasn't the time or place to tell her, but the twins knew exactly what had happened. The previous day, Milo and Sadie had walked into the DA's office and handed them a thumb drive full of evidence that they themselves had only viewed a portion of.

When the twins started high school, Milo inherited an old laptop from Jarvis. Milo was more of an expert at technology than his father, so he had taken the time to clear files, remove old downloads, and reset the computer to factory settings. He had also made sure to back up his dad's old files on an external hard drive, something he remembered only after the trial had begun. News reports made it sound as if Morgan was trying to cry "self-defense" because of her own guilt, but Milo knew better. He had lost one parent and refused to lose another.

When Milo remembered the hard drive, he debated not telling his sister, but that was impossible to comprehend. So, together one evening, they snuck into their dad's house, dug through box after box of their parents' belongings, and finally hit a stroke of luck when they found the hard drive.

As they plugged it into Sadie's computer, they only made it past one file and two videos before realizing they had a gold mine. A disgusting, nasty, horrifying gold mine. They downloaded as much as they could onto the USB stick and carried it straight to the DA's office. The attorneys notified police, who combed through evidence of Jarvis drugging and coaxing Morgan into compromising positions throughout their marriage, receipts of solicitations for sex on Craigslist, copies of emails extorting his business partner and investors, and so much more. While none of it explained what exactly happened in that parking lot, they were far more inclined to believe Morgan's explanation of events after watching Jarvis' horrific behavior firsthand.

And the world would never even know. One thing the attorneys, police, and judge all agreed on was that the public spectacle around the murder case had reached a fever pitch. If any of this information was released, it was highly possible the narrative would shift and the police would be accused of botching the investigation. After all, why did children find the evidence and not the police? How had they not seen Jarvis for what he was? They all wanted to avoid the bad press that would surely follow the release of salacious details, as well as potential lawsuits. It was unlikely Morgan would sue the county—it was clear she just wanted to get on with her life—but it was all but inevitable that Emily Connor would go after the government. And with her massive resources behind her, a civil lawsuit would be both time-consuming and expensive, two things the county could *not* afford.

The DA's office also knew the twins wanted to protect their mother. No child wants their father's horrific abuse and shady business dealings on display for the world to see, and Sadie and Milo had been put through the wringer. Morgan and her children were ready to move on. DA Bondar didn't hesitate to leverage this fact when negotiating a deal with the twins: Morgan's charges would be dropped and none of the data would be released to the public. In return, the extended Connor family would be unable to sue, and none of their father's horrific actions would be made public. It was a win-win.

So, as the sun hung high in the morning sky, Morgan walked out of the county court, freer than she had ever been in her adult life.

"Hey! I need your address," Shannon said as Morgan picked up her phone with a *hello*.

"Um, hey! How's it going?" Morgan laughed. "It's been a minute since we chatted."

"Ah, you know me. All business," Shannon chuckled. "How are you, my friend? Yours is still the craziest case I've ever been part of."

"Yeah, you haven't had any other exciting murder trials since me?" Morgan teased. "I feel so special."

"I'll stick to divorce, thanks," Shannon assured her. "And speaking of which, yours is, well, final."

"Um, what?" Morgan asked, shocked that Shannon would bring up her divorce now, more than three years after Jarvis' death.

"Listen, I know it sounds crazy, but the Connors must have done some maneuvering. I just got the mail, and I am looking at an envelope that holds your certificate of divorce, proving that it is, in fact, final. Plus a *fat* check, my friend."

"A check?"

"Yep. So, I need your new address. How's Idaho anyway?" Shannon asked.

"Colorful," Morgan sighed pensively. "You should see the colors here, Shan."

"Well, maybe I should hand deliver this one," Shannon said. Morgan could practically hear her smile through the phone and it fully warmed her heart. She didn't have words to express the gratitude she felt for Shannon.

"You're welcome anytime," Morgan sincerely replied.

"Okay, actually, why not?" she said, "I really should come see you. That would be amazing! How are the kids doing?"

"Well, Milo's at the University of Oregon, and Sadie's with me for now. She's going to the University of Iowa here and living at home. I'm trying to get her to fly the nest a little and enjoy campus life, but she still watches out for me pretty closely," Morgan smiled. "They both do."

"Well, that's good. I'm glad that they had access to their college funds. I was worried for a bit there. And speaking of which, I've got a few million here that'll help."

"*What?*" Morgan was genuinely clueless.

"Yeah, this check..." Shannon struggled to explain over the phone. "Emily issued a payment for over eight million dollars, Morgan."

"I don't understand," Morgan gasped.

"I don't quite get it myself," Shannon admitted. "All I can think of is that Emily may have filed a complaint with the county after the DA dropped the charges against you and found out the truth. She knows the DA has damning evidence of Jarvis' abuse. Evidence you could decide to go public with someday. Not that you would, but I can guess that's how Emily's mind works. No doubt she would use it for blackmail if the roles were reversed."

"As you know," she continued, "I petitioned for your alimony and child support from Jarvis' estate, but Emily had claimed his funds pretty swiftly. Anyway, Aimee's lawyer had communicated that his additional assets were all tied up in legal negotiations, but I recently heard that everything is settled. So, I'm guessing this is your payoff. They're basically saying, 'Don't ever talk to or about us again.'" Shannon explained.

"Gladly," Morgan admitted. "And it only cost them eight million dollars!" she chuckled.

Three years to the day Morgan walked out of court in ultimate freedom, she entered a sprawling ranch with stables, three houses, a barn, and a small lake covering seventy acres.

"This is where you could have your instructors hold classes," Cindy, the real estate agent who helped Morgan find an apartment near Sadie's college campus, was now leading her through the property, pointing to one of the smaller homes. "And the big house is perfect for retreats. It's already set up for that kind of thing with en suites in each room."

"It's perfect," Morgan smiled. "I'll take it," she declared.

"Well, there are two other properties I have to show you," Cindy explained.

"No, it's this one. I can feel it."

"Well, you got it," Cindy shrugged, happy to close the sale. "I'll just need to make a few calls."

Morgan walked down the path, past the old house and toward a line of towering pines. Her vision of offering a retreat space for healing was coming to life. With half of the money she received from her settlement, Morgan would be able to buy the ranch and still make necessary renovations, get licenses, and hire the professionals needed to provide care for women and children who had suffered abuse.

Tiffany and Morgan had spent the previous month establishing a nonprofit with the state of Idaho and Tiffany was making the cross-country move in less than a week. Her nursing experience was invaluable to the process and the connections she had made in her career allowed the women to find the exact people and resources needed to establish a fully-operational facility. It wasn't a perfect ending to their story; it was a perfect new beginning.

ABOUT THE AUTHOR

 Shelly Snow Pordea is renowned as a speaker, publishing consultant, and author of the captivating *Tracing Time* trilogy. This trilogy, a compelling narrative of women navigating the complexities of life while endeavoring to protect themselves and their loved ones, has consistently ranked among the top one hundred Time Travel Romance books on Amazon Kindle, attesting to its widespread popularity.

In addition to her success in fiction, Shelly has ventured into the realm of children's literature with her debut book, *The Hug Who Had No Arms,* an instant #1 bestseller on Amazon. Crafted during the pandemic to address the challenges of social distancing, this heartwarming tale encourages families to embrace unique differences and express love in diverse ways. Shelly's commitment to inclusivity is evident in the multilingual versions of the book, currently available in

Romanian, Persian, and Spanish, reflecting her dedication to reaching a global audience.

Beyond her literary achievements, Shelly is a courageous advocate for survivors of spiritual, sexual, and institutional abuse. Drawing from her own experiences as a cult survivor and victim of childhood sexual abuse, she utilizes the power of storytelling to effect change. As a screenwriter, Shelly collaborates with her brother, talented actor Jon Snow, in the production of a fictional adaptation for a series drama based on their personal story to shed light on coercive control and manipulation while amplifying the voices of those who have faced similar challenges. She is a proud Board Member of the nonprofit Living Cult Free.

As a publishing expert, Shelly offers online courses for the self-starter, as well as consultations for small businesses, nonprofits, and corporations. Find more about her work at shellysnowpordea.com.

Beyond her professional pursuits, Shelly is a dedicated mother to three incredible adults, loving wife to her favorite guy, George, for nearly three decades, and Buni (boo-nee) to one enchanting, magical granddaughter. She invites you to join her journey on social media, where she shares her insights and creative endeavors. Follow her @shellysnowpordea.

ALSO BY
SHELLY SNOW PORDEA

Book 1 in the *Tracing Time Trilogy*, Anna Wright grapples with the effects of her depression while living a secluded life with her young family abroad. When her husband disappears, she is faced with accepting the assumption of his death or uncovering the truth behind his work.

Anna returns to the only thing she knows, her Midwest family, but life on the farm isn't like what it was growing up. Times and people have changed, and her quest to find herself again turns into a burning desire to know the truth. Her husband's colleague, Christopher, and the distinguished Professor Trinkton reveal secrets behind their studies, leaving Anna with the impossible choice to either join their efforts or lose David forever.

While she is an involved and loving mother, she does the unthinkable, choosing to travel through space and time without her children, justifying to herself that she's on a mission to help save the planet and return her husband safely to his family. Her tenacity and determination lead her to successfully embark on an unfathomable journey. And what she finds is unthinkable: her husband, stuck in a time period in which he was unable to access the technology needed to return, has been betrothed to another.

The Victorian British era in which David had been trapped for nearly eight years left him all but hopeless until Anna arrives. Overcoming the epic trials their true love story must face, along with a mystical guide, together they make a way to return. But things aren't simple when toying with the fabric of time.

Book 2 in the *Tracing Time Trilogy*. Fourteen years after the disappearance of David and Anna, Christopher Mack is imprisoned for their murders. Maggie Sturgeon, the young daughter who was left behind had been raised by her mother's brother and Turkish-born auntie, Ami.

Now an adult, Maggie finds that Trinkton, who she knew to be the lawyer involved in the murder case, was actually her parents' former Professor at UCLA. Following in her father's footsteps and being accepted into their science program, she too finds herself uncovering secrets she was never meant to know.

Connecting with a fellow student, and son of a prominent professor himself, Maggie and Rowan join forces to unearth every mystery about the past. What they didn't expect was to be entangled far more than they could have imagined. Rowan finds that his parents were also participants in the infamous time travel program as they uncover a convoluted string of events that led them to become deeply involved in a network of people in *The Program.*

Arriving in 1970s England, they reunite with their parents only to be plunged into a world from which they only wished they could escape. Maggie and Rowan ultimately believe they can make a difference by trying to thwart the growing effects of climate change, but their compromise is being fully controlled by *The Company.*

The family drama an absentee parent must face with their adult children takes on new meaning once Maggie confronts her parents as their paths cross in a time period none of them were meant to experience.

Book 3 in *The Tracing Time Trilogy.* After years in *The Program,* two generations of parents who had struggled to make sense of the lives they built were forced to reveal secrets to yet another generation. Young Maisy had a peaceful life growing up in England as the daughter of expats in the 1990s, but her stoic personality and stunning looks always drew attention. Thinking it was her weirdness that made her feel like she never quite fit in and determined to find herself, she set off on a backpacking adventure that would change her life.

Antonio was unlike anyone she'd ever met. Dropping her a secret note in an airport lounge, he leads Maisy to a startling discovery of who she really was, no spiritual self-revelation involved. Coming to terms with the fact that she was the third generation in a family of time travelers, Maisy conspires with Antonio to blow the whole thing up. She finally feels like she has answers for her misfit life, yet she has only scratched the surface.

Being involved with *The Company* has taken its toll on everyone, and Maisy is the young blood needed to lead the charge for this family to regain their freedom once and for all. While not fully abandoning the initial mission of trying to help save the planet, she, her parents, and grandparents set off to do collectively what one could not accomplish alone. One problem remains for Maisy, Antonio isn't part of the family.

Leaving the past behind, all three generations duly return to the twenty-first century as Trinkton and Christopher are finally able to share the truth about what had transpired during their absence. Both happy endings and love lost are inevitable.

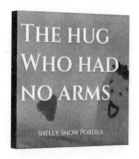

Inspired by the pandemic, a time when the world seemed to stop hugging, author Shelly Snow Pordea took to her love of drawing and storytelling to create a children's tale that will warm any heart. Join this lovely friend as he finds that, even though he was born without arms, the warmth of his love can be felt in many ways. Perfect for parents and children coping with the strange practices of social distancing or overall anxiety with physical expression. Share the joy of knowing that we can show our love in various ways, and with whatever tools we are given.

"This book, like the title suggests, feels like a warm embrace—and one we desperately need right now."

—**Jeff Goins**, bestselling author and father

"During a time when so many of us feel unable to show love the way we would like to, Shelly Snow Pordea's precious words weave a world where children (and grown-up children, too) are reminded that love comes in all shapes, sizes and forms, and what really matters is that we share it."

—**Seven Sinclaire,** poet and mental health advocate

Bilingual versions of *The Hug Who Had No Arms* available in Romanian, Persian, and Spanish.

As editor and contributing author in this anthology, Shelly shares a glimpse into her life story in the chapter entitled, *Follow the Yellow Brick Road.* In *Success Matters: Strong Women Making a Difference in Business and Community,* thirteen captivating and influential women come together to share inspiring stories about the remarkable impact strong businesswomen have on society.

Within the pages of this powerful anthology, each author unveils their unique perspective on success, highlighting how they are not only shaping individual enterprises but also influencing and transforming communities while embracing their social responsibility.